In *Christ and Chaos*, Gerald Borchert tackles a host of pressing ethical issues from a biblical perspective. Always irenic and focused on the love of God for humans and humans' love for one another, Borchert sees ethics as dealing with the pervasive chaos prevalent in the world, including contemporary culture. The topics he addresses—from equality to eternity to divorce and remarriage to what it means to be a Christian—are relevant and handled with the care of an expert surgeon. This engaging and lively book deserves to be read and studied by anyone who wants to know and live by what the Bible teaches about life in the twenty-first century.

Eric W. Bolger
Vice President for Academic Affairs
Dean and Professor of Philosophy-Religion
College of the Ozarks

I truly like the concept of this book. "Change is inevitable. You either change or you become irrelevant." This statement has increasingly come to represent contemporary thinking. But how do Christians and the Christian church with its time-honored truths respond to this milieu? Borchert understands what we are all facing and the confusion and chaos that have resulted from too much change—and such rapid change at that! Many long-held values, traditions, practices, and beliefs are under increasing attack. There is a desperate need for guidance from trusted and experienced thinkers who understand the Bible and its message. As a leader in the Christian community for many years, Borchert is the ideal person to help us grapple with issues that perplex us all and he does so by leading us to understand that grace, not dogmatism, enables us to be "children of light" amidst the darkness that surrounds us. Every topic in this book is of utmost relevance to being a Christian in today's world, but the issues are presented in a warm and caring manner that seeks the leading of the Spirit rather than confrontation and controversy. For that reason alone, this book is a must read.

Harry H. Hiller
Director, Cities and the Olympics Project
Faculty Professor of Urban Sociology
University of Calgary

In this extraordinary volume, "Dr. B" Borchert provides us with a wise pastoral response to the questions that churches ask pastors and our culture asks Christians. He approaches difficult issues in a way that combines his love for the Lord, his wit as a teacher, his deep knowledge of the Bible, and his role as a parent. He explains difficult topics conversationally—like a father to a son and a pastor to his friends. Dr. B courageously addresses complex topics the way the book of Proverbs equips future generations—from parent to child. He avoids clichés and sound bites and provides biblical truth for pastors and believers to use whether they are at the Lord's table or at the kitchen table. He addresses cultural and political issues the way Jesus dealt with argumentative Pharisees—with story, grace, humor, and insight. He probes us with questions of which we had not thought until we read the book, and we learn even more about his remarkable journey as a follower of Jesus. *Christ and Chaos* calms the stormy waters of Christian conflict by providing helpful conversation starters that allow us to listen, grow, and reconcile others to Christ.

William D. Shiell
President
Professor of Pastoral Theology
Northern Baptist Theological Seminary

Christ and Chaos is a bold book that does not view the person and work of Jesus Christ as distinctly isolated from the chaos of our twenty-first-century world. Thankfully, author Gerald Borchert places them together where they belong. Christ is not afraid of chaos, and chaos continually confronts Christ. This is the realization that can speak volumes in our broken world. Borchert does not offer easy answers, but insightful questions that, in turn, lead the reader to deeper understanding and faithful living. His brilliance as a world-class New Testament scholar combined with the love of a spiritual father is a rare combination that makes this book stand apart. I recommend it to anyone desiring to face courageously the ethical issues of this generation with both human intelligence and Christian grace.

Constance M. Cherry
Professor of Worship and Pastoral Ministry
School of Theology and Ministry
Indiana Wesleyan University

I give the chapter on homosexuality very high marks. Borchert is highly respectful of Scripture and tradition; keenly aware of ongoing discoveries in human makeup; kindly insistent on a gracious orthopraxy calling believers to treat all persons lovingly, as Jesus would; prudently subtle, yet unmistakably Jesus-like in his approach to the issue and response to the vulnerable in our midst. History will smile kindly on the fair treatment of a difficult matter. Superb work!

Randall O'Brien
President
Professor of Old Testament
Carson-Newman University

Gerald Borchert has a long history of writing books relevant to the church in the current generation. *Christ and Chaos* is no different. Through a series of letters to his pastor sons and "friends," Borchert takes up a whole host of ethical questions that contemporary Christians and non-Christians are asking today, from equality to marriage and divorce to homosexuality to Christians and government among others. Drawing upon decades of Scripture study, teaching in theological schools, participation in church and society, and his legal training, Borchert has crafted a book of questions and answers that show a great deal of wisdom, humility, and faithfulness to Scripture. Some of the "answers" are tentative, leading the reader into further questions, but Borchert desires for his readers to engage the questions, the Christian Scriptures, and people in dialogue, to move toward a faithful and ethical approach to life and the chaos that face us every day.

R. Jackson Painter
Professor of New Testament
Simpson University

Christ and Chaos is a very insightful book, addressing many current issues that confront Christians. Focused around a series of questions addressed to his two sons and his readers identified as "friends," Borchert's responses are based on a lifetime of personal, pastoral, and teaching experiences that are steeped in biblical analysis and understanding. He is candid and transparent concerning the thorny issues to which he calls Christians as we seek understanding and the "transforming power of God that overcomes pettiness, selfishness, and conflict." His responses on how to apply biblical principles to our divisive political situations provide pertinent, practical advice on the way Christians should interact with current circumstances and how to apply biblical principles to our thoughts and actions. Employing both Old Testament and New Testament teachings, he explains how to approach the stigma often associated with divorce from a biblically informed position. He also supplies a well-reasoned and cautionary way to deal with the highly controversial issue of homosexuality. Throughout the work his questions are insightful and his thoughtful responses are perceptive and well-reasoned. He is eminently fair-minded, biblical, and Christlike in his explanations, while challenging readers to think through their own views on the issues confronting contemporary society.

Charles W. Weber
Emeritus Professor of History
Wheaton College

Some of the greatest scholars in history, from Socrates to Aquinas and beyond, have used pressing questions as the source and even architecture of their work. Asking questions and seeking answers is the foundation of sound critical thinking, the scientific method, even fruitful political discourse. Renowned biblical scholar Gerald L. Borchert employs this time-tested method to wrestle with complex ethical and moral questions facing our world today. Written as a father to his sons and friends, Borchert takes a compassionate, thoughtful, and principled pastoral approach, stimulating the reader to ask more questions about the issues he raises. He looks for biblically rooted responses that provide guidance, some practical and concrete, but some requiring an appropriate sacrificial commitment to following Jesus in the paths of righteousness, peace, joy, and love of God and humankind. This kind of discipleship and formation into Christlikeness is at the heart of worship renewal.

James H. Hart
President
Robert E. Webber Institute for Worship Studies

Christ and Chaos reveals Gerald Borchert's heart for God and his desire for the church to be a place that exhibits the love of God. His conclusions sparked in me conversations about the nature of faith, the redemptive work of Christ, and the role we as followers of Christ play in God's mission. Borchert is one of those scholars who can connect the study of God's Word to the pastoral work of walking alongside others. Given the chaos around us, entering into a conversation about Christ in the midst of that chaos is something for which each of us should yearn! Dr. Borchert is a good conversation partner to have on the journey.

Greg Henson
President
Sioux Falls Seminary

Christ and Chaos offers concise responses to a host of ethical and philosophical questions that arise in discussions among contemporary Christians. As a veteran New Testament scholar and master teacher, Borchert draws on serious scholarship and experienced dialogue with both beginning and advanced students to formulate his interaction with the questions selected for this work. Encounter with its contents will greatly deepen the conversation.

Charles Scalise
Senior Professor of Church History
Fuller Theological Seminary

Using his "teaching handle," Dr. B shares his life-learning in the style of personal letters to his sons and friends. Unlike how C.S. Lewis' *Screwtape* gives advice to his young protégé Wormwood, Dr. Borchert's approach in *Christ and Chaos* is, among other things, biblically founded, critically reflective, pastorally focused, carefully nuanced, socially relevant, and respectful of diverse viewpoints. Although containing many delicious appetizers, there is here a plethora of compact yet dense meals that satisfy one's appetite for understanding how best to live a Christ-like life in a world of chaos and conflict. This is solid food, not fast food. It is founded on the solid meat of the Word, providing well-aged analyses that derive from a lifetime of preparation and application. Humbly sharing wisdom, his style equips believers to engage others respectfully and knowledgeably through dialogue, not diatribe, in hopes of building greater societal peace, security, and order.

Ralph Korner
Dean and Associate Professor of Biblical Studies
Taylor Seminary

Gerald L. Borchert

CHRIST

and

CHAOS

Biblical Keys to Ethical Questions

© 2020

Published in the United States by Nurturing Faith Inc., Macon GA,
www.nurturingfaith.net.

Library of Congress Cataloging-in-Publication Data is available.

ISBN: 978-1-63528-088-3

All translations of the biblical texts in this work have been rendered from the Hebrew and Greek texts
by the author, although he readily admits his thought processes have been influenced considerably by a
combination of the King James and Revised Standard versions of the Bible. The nuances and his understandings, however, are his.

Webber Institute Books

Webber Institute Books (WIB) serves as the publishing arm of the Robert E. Webber Institute for Worship Studies (IWS). The Institute was founded by the late Robert E. Webber for the purpose of forming servant leaders in worship renewal with the perspective that "the way to the future necessarily runs through the past." IWS is the only school in North America dedicated solely to graduate education in biblical foundations, historical development, theological reflection, and cultural analysis of worship. Its vision emphasizes that its graduates will "participate intentionally in the story of the Triune God" in order to "bring renewal in the local and global church by shaping life and ministry according to that story." In scope it is "gospel-centered in nature and ecumenical in outlook, embracing and serving the whole church in its many expressions and variations." Those interested in obtaining further information concerning the Institute should consult www.iws.edu.

Webber Institute books are published by agreement with Nurturing Faith (www. nurturingfaith.net) to provide a means for disseminating to the general public varying and differing views concerning the many aspects of worship and Christian life. The ideas expressed in these published materials wholly remain the views of the authors themselves and are not necessarily those of IWS or the publisher.

It is the prayerful concern of both IWS and WIB that the information contained in these works will stimulate further reflection and discussion. The results of such exchange of ideas hopefully will enhance worship renewal within the various segments of the Christian church. Moreover, in keeping with the hopes and dreams of founder Bob Webber, may all that is done through this publishing enterprise enable Christians to reject the narcissistic patterns prevalent in contemporary society and give the glory to God who sent Jesus, the Christ, to provide for human transformation and in concert provided humans with the divine triune presence through the Holy Spirit.

Robert Myers
General Editor

Gerald L. Borchert
Founding Editor

James Hart
President, IWS

Other Works by Gerald L. Borchert

Today's Model Church
(Roger Williams Press, 1971)

Dynamics of Evangelism
(Word Books, 1976)

Paul and His Interpreters, TSF–IBR
(InterVarsity, 1985)

Spiritual Dimensions of Pastoral Care
(Westminster Press, 1985)

Discovering Thessalonians
(Guideposts, 1986)

Assurance and Warning
(Broadman Press, 1986;
Word N Works, 2006)

The Crisis of Fear
(Broadman Press, 1988)

"John" in *Mercer Commentary on the Bible*
(Mercer University Press, 1995, 1996)

"John 1–11," "John 12–21"
in *New American Commentary*
(Broadman & Holman, 1996, 2002)

"Galatians" in *Romans and Galatians,*
Cornerstone Biblical Commentary
(Tyndale House, 2007)

Worship in the New Testament:
Divine Mystery and Human Response
(Chalice Press, 2008)

"Revelation" in *NLT Study Bible*
(Tyndale House, 2008, 2017)

Jesus of Nazareth:
Background, Witnesses, and Significance
(Mercer University Press, 2011)

Assaulted by Grief:
Finding God in Broken Places
(Mossy Creek Press, 2011)

The Lands of the Bible: Israel, the Palestinian
Territories, Sinai & Egypt, Jordan,
Notes on Syria and Lebanon,
Comments on the Arab-Israeli Wars and the
Palestinian Refugees, The Clash of Cultures
(Mossy Creek Press, 2011)

The Lands of the Bible:
In the Footsteps of Paul and John
(Mossy Creek Press, 20012)

Portraits of Jesus for an
Age of Biblical Illiteracy
(Smyth & Helwys, 2016)

"Galatians," "Romans" in *New Living Translation*
(Tyndale House, 1996, 2004, etc.)

Contents

Acknowledgments

I am sincerely indebted to my oldest son, Mark, who field-tested many of my questions and answers in his church while I had the opportunity to observe the interaction with the members in those sessions.

You will also note that I sent my writing to scholars from representative disciplines and various representative schools to ask for their responses to my work. I have attached their impressions at the beginning of this work. I am deeply indebted to them for their responses.

I prayerfully trust that you, the readers, will find my work to be stimulating and that the questions herein will push you to reflect even more on the questions concerning life that I have proposed. I welcome your responses, and I offer here a preliminary "Thank you" for any reflections you might be willing to share with me.

Of course, you will quickly recognize that I have a great indebtedness to my dear wife and companion, Doris, who has been my authentic partner in our family for many years as well as being a professor of Christian education—and I rejoice and am grateful that she continues to support me in my writing and teaching.

I also thank both of our two sons, Mark and Tim, who are the focus of my letters in this work. Both of them have constantly inspired us to be more authentic parents and they have asked innumerable questions in the course of these years. Not only have they posed their queries, but they also have genuinely helped us as parents in negotiating our answers. We watched them carefully as they sought to navigate their lives and as they have matured in their understanding of theology and life. "Thank you," sons, for your immeasurable contributions to us as parents.

Then to our grandchildren—Elissa, Tim Jr., Seth, and Jessica—who are quickly assuming their roles in the next generation of adults, I dedicate this book to you with the prayer that each of you will continue to allow the Holy Spirit with the model of Jesus be the GPS for your decisions in life. And what I pray for the four of you, I especially pray for all young adults who have said an initial "yes" to Jesus and struggle to discover what that commitment means in the context of a world that is hurling questions at humans faster than answers seem to be available. Just remember that God's Spirit is very much alive and desires to guide you into all truth (John 16:13).

Finally, I am grateful beyond words to both the editorial committee of Webber Institute Books for the unanimous approval of including my work in their Worship and Spirituality publications, as well as to the editors and production people at Nurturing Faith Inc. who have transformed my manuscript into a distinguished product.

A genuine "Thanks" to each of you for your kind spirit and dedicated work!

Biblical Keys to Ethical Questions[1]

The Pervasiveness of Questions

Questions, Questions! Our world and our lives are filled with questions. Questions are at the heart of education. Perceptive students are filled with questions. Just try being a parent and attempting to escape being bombarded with the question, "Why?" You cannot be a person and not ask questions about the significance of your relationships. You cannot be a human and not have questions about life and its meaning. You cannot be a Christian and not have questions about God—indeed about the implications for how God works in the world and how you should live with God. Actually, questions frame our lives and motivate who we are and how we act.

Most people on earth have questions as they long for security, peace, and order. Yet this world is not a fairytale land. We may be wishing for a "live happily ever after" story to life but such a reality, the Bible says, awaits the new heaven and the new earth when the former things have passed away (Rev. 21:1). In the meantime, as we seek to live in our world where chaos and evil abound, we usually have scores of questions because genuine order to life and long-lasting tranquility are often hard to find. Even when we try to relax, our movies and television programs blast us with confusion, war, and violence—to say nothing of our daily news reports.

We may play a video clip of running water on our cell phones to calm our shattered nerves and stop those incessant questions, but we quickly thereafter awaken to the presence of chaos and confusion. It is, moreover, fascinating that our television sponsors have now come to recognize the reality of disorder that is present in most people's lives and offer programs on how to clean up the clutter of our homes. Questions are inevitable when we seek to understand the chaos in our world and in our lives. And chaos raises the question of order and of ethical integrity.

Some readers will quickly recognize in *Christ and Chaos* that I interweave theological and ethical concerns. I would just as quickly respond that you are correct, but I would hasten to add that my main concern is not with doing traditional theology. Instead, my basic concern is with the task of living out the implications of our theology, and that is the reason I have focused this work primarily on ethical questions.

The Problem of Chaos and God's Goal of Harmony

Thus, although God has endowed humans with the gift of freedom, we seem to gravitate to chaos rather than order and to conflict rather than harmony. Families, communities, and nations that are known for harmony and integrity are often rare to find so that if and when we discover a modicum of both, they provide inspiration for our troubled world—and yes, a sound byte about such harmony and order might even make the evening news in the midst of all the troubles that are ever present.

Harmony is built upon love and caring and is sadly missing in our world today—but it is desperately needed, especially in our contemporary shattered existence. Although we may think that our current generations are more sophisticated and able to handle the challenges of life better than earlier ones, we may be more in need of psychosomatic assistance than the ancients because of our hollowness and fragmentation as humans.

So, I suggest that we ponder both the many questions I have in this little work and not dismiss too quickly the secret that lies just under the surface in the model command that Jesus gave to his disciples to love one another (John 13:34-35). There is, I suggest, much more hidden in that imperative than we may want to admit. It certainly is related to many of the issues of life that trouble us as humans. And strange as it may seem, in our narcissistic, me-centered society harmony, order, and integrity are actually regarded as "good news" because we all can sense that our current reality is badly shaken, broken, frustrated, anxious, divisive, and conflict-oriented.

Although the church of Jesus from the beginning was supposed to be known by love and what the New Testament calls *koinonia* (fellowship or community), I must sadly admit that sometimes it also models disorder and conflict while mouthing words of love and integrity. In spite of its human brokenness, the church does have a message for our chaotic world: God who made the world actually loves the world! That love is not merely a Greek virtue. Nor is that message merely a sugar coating on our fractured reality. Rather, it is the most authentic message on this planet. In plain, unvarnished truth the message is that God actually sent his one and only Son to make a radical difference in this perplexing strife-torn world. That historical mission of God's envoy has been and continues to be genuinely transformative and actually regenerative.

Through this Son, God seeks to initiate a radical change in the perspectives of humans from self-centeredness to God-centeredness. This change is rooted in the unfathomable love that God has for humanity, and it is often mysteriously hidden or tucked among many of those members who compose Christ's body, which we call the church, and who seek diligently to model integrity in their lives as caring humans. Some of them may be poor, weak and unheralded, but they are stalwart models of ethical maturity.

The Reality of Human Frailty and the Divine Plan

In making this claim for such people in the Christian community, I admit that churches are mere human institutions and that Christians are beset with the inner turmoil and frustrations present in the wider humanity. Their members are very human in dealing with the questions about their reality. Yet I frequently discover striking examples of authentic love and order tucked in a Christian community that are born not out of human effort but out of the transforming power of God that overcomes pettiness, selfishness, and conflict. Furthermore, I firmly believe that humans do not need to live continually in a state of chaos because when they become correctly oriented to God, chaos can often mysteriously give way to the initiation of more order, harmony, and community. That is the reason I have sought here to publish some of my thoughts that were originally directed to my sons, Mark and Tim. I offer these thoughts now to you who are other members of God's children in Christ and to those who might just be intrigued to find out a little more about God's pattern for living above the chaos in our world.

For those who might be doubters or who think I might be in danger of presenting a rose-colored picture of the church, I would counter with: Just read my thoughts and you will soon realize that I am very much aware of the warts and wrinkles in the church. It is hardly perfect. It is indeed very human and frail. But mysteriously, when not expected, the Christian community can often surprise us at just how authentic, loving, and caring its people can be. So, when I critique the church and enumerate its weakness and participation in chaos, please recognize that I nevertheless thank God for birthing me into this marvelous company that is one of the great mysteries in the world. When the church seems to be at its weakest, often then its people are revealed in their strength and vitality because then they become most dependent on their Master. So I welcome you to join me in pursuing the many vexing questions that confront our faith communities as we wrestle with difficult ethical (perhaps for you also theological) questions as we attempt to live authentically with Christ in the context of chaos—which surely enfolds all of us, both Christians and those who might wonder what it means to follow Christ.

The Author's Pilgrimage to Meaning and the Purpose of This Work

Concerning the authorship of this work, I should tell you briefly that I am a former lawyer and have been a pastor of both large and small churches, a seminary professor, an educational administrator, and a university professor. During nearly a decade I had the privilege of trying to answer scores of questions in a regular print forum for a Christian denomination while I was a dean in one of its seminaries. I must admit that I often brought home those questions and tried to think out my answers in our family context with my dear wife, who also has been a seminary professor, and with our two sons, both of whom have subsequently become pastors and have also occupied other roles. I usually attempted to anticipate many of their probing queries, but I was not always prepared for the depth to which they would push me in my responses. That, of course, is the joy of being a parent and seeking to answer questions.

During our sons' earlier years, we as a family read many books together so our sons were very familiar with their role of asking questions. Seeking answers to those questions has been one of the great experiences for our family, and it continues to be such when we get together or talk by phone. Please join me in considering at least some of the scores of questions I have raised in this work and that I believe can be crucial for our growth and maturing as Christians.

Some of the questions you may have already considered and answered to your satisfaction for the present. Some of them may challenge your presuppositions or your earlier conclusions and may need to be reconsidered. Some of the questions may require that you obtain further insight or information in order to be answered satisfactorily. Some of them may prove to be a little unsettling at the present time or may appear from your point of view to be very difficult to answer, and thus may have to remain tentative much longer.

Even though we are merely human and do not have complete answers in our search for meaning to these and other issues of life, wrestling with their potential answers can lead all of us into a more authentic understanding of the ethical realities of life. And by the way, the world—especially the church—needs us to wrestle with such questions so that we can move beyond the simplistic answers that are frequently suggested by those around us. In turn, reflecting on them should help us to recognize the incredible nature of having been created by God to be responsible humans. I love to watch my students wrestle with such questions because I realize that the world and the church will be the recipients of their struggles, especially in this era when most of our answers are given to us in sound bytes on television or in brief snippets in text messages on our cell phones!

With this background in mind, it should not be a great surprise to you that after having written more than a score of books and several hundred articles I continue to ask wrenching questions related to crucial ethical and theological issues in life. These questions seem to flow readily to my mind—and I trust to your mind also. So, like many teachers before me, seeking answers to questions usually brings other questions. That is the reason I have written this book and why I love teaching and trying to stimulate searching minds—especially among able younger thinkers. These younger minds simply push me beyond my previous conclusions. Accordingly, to my students throughout the years—and many others—I stand in deep gratitude for generating in me the desire to learn from them and hopefully from you too. Please feel free to contact me at gdborchert@aol.com whether you agree or disagree with me or have comments. I would be grateful to receive your questions.

The Methodology and Organization of the Book

While I am not attached to any particular method of interpretation, I have always found that the Wesleyan quadrilateral is a fairly wholesome manner of approaching questions. I take the Bible very seriously and reckon with its contextual framework, especially the pattern of Jesus in reaching understanding. Then I take seriously what tradition has to say about a matter. Moreover, I ask how reasonable is my thinking and how does my view deal authentically not only with my personal experience but also with general human experience up to the current time. Therefore, you will note that I have given you many experiences besides biblical citations in this work. If we take all of these four elements into account, our conclusions are likely to be close to the truth. Failure to neglect any one of them will likely lead to a skewed view of reality. Yet concerning any answers we might offer, we must always remember that we are not divine—we are merely human!

You will quickly realize that in this work I have chosen to discuss a number of difficult and disputed issues that have been troubling for not a few Christians. Some issues may have been a concern for you or for those outside the Christian church. Other people may even wonder why Christians should be concerned about them. But I can assure you that they are not superficial issues. I have also added a number of questions at the end of each section to stimulate your further pondering of these issues. These additional questions can be used as thought stimulators in the context of an academic class or a dialogue group, or indeed for personal reflection. I hope you will discuss these questions seriously with others as you strive to arrive at authentically Christlike answers for life.

For convenience, I have divided my questions into fourteen segments plus a major postscript on other crucial issues that may push you into considering where our world may be heading in the foreseeable future. I trust that the questions can actually serve you as thought-provokers. I have used many of them in my various courses in biblical theology. Moreover, my elder son, Mark (who is the chair of the communications department at a university and a pastor), kindly agreed to field-test these topics and questions with a study group in his church in which I had the privilege of being mostly an observer so that I too could learn well.

I make no claim that my views in this book are the only relevant words on the subjects herein treated, but I think the questions are worthy of serious reflection. Since my focus is primarily on the questions, I have tried to avoid citing endless sources as I have done throughout my academic life. My goal has been to stimulate you, the reader, to reflect not only on the questions but also on the biblical texts cited and on my experiences. Both should stimulate you to reflect further on how you make important life decisions concerning ethical and theological issues and about how you deal with the implications that flow from those decisions. Furthermore, since I continue to address such questions to my ordained sons and their families, I have addressed these questions and answers in our familiar letter format to my two sons, Mark and Tim, but have added "Friends" to include you the readers.

I trust you will recognize that in my organization I move from chaos through multiple issues and then to the Dark Side and the recognition of the reality of evil before I deal with the terminal issues of death, heaven, and eternity. I end with worship because I firmly believe that for a Christian—who lives on this revolving planet in the vastness of space—worship relates not merely to attending church and "worship services" or practicing various disciplines, but involves all of life. Therefore, worship is a crucial element in approaching ethical integrity.

Before I reach my conclusion and at the suggestion of a former doctoral student, I would add another issue concerning my teaching. I am a Christian theologian who is prepared to live with tension. Many Christians are uncomfortable with tension and are anxious to eliminate alternatives. They try to settle for one option and thereby tend—like all of us—to skew theological realities. I am prepared to live with tension because we are not omniscient. In theology some favor grace over faith, the divine over the human or the reverse. But I believe that the answer to understanding salvation and other matters of Christian thought and life actually lies within the tension between the human and the divine. Christian theology, ethics, and life involve both the wise, caring God and frail, sinful humans. I believe that the more we learn to build our theologies and ethics on that inherent tension, the more we will reach satisfying theological constructs.

Conclusion

Finally, I invite you to join my wife and me on our pilgrimage in which we seek, as best we can, to "walk" with the Lord as humble servants and not as authoritarian purveyors of absolute directives. We are not inerrant in our messaging, but we have lived with God for a long time and have seen a great deal of pain and hurt as well as frothy Christianity and false piety that claim to be "God-inspired" but melts in the heat of trouble, confusion, and suffering. Therefore, in this book I have sought as much as possible to be honest and forthright in communicating to you my sincere thoughts and experiences concerning some of the wrenching issues I have discussed here. I pray that God will be with you as you read and reflect on my words. And please remember: Wrestling with questions can be a fruitful path to wisdom!

Note

[1]As you read this work, please bear in mind this prefatory statement: I am focusing this book on questions related to ethical issues for this generation of text-messaging readers. I am not attempting to provide full reference notes or a complete bibliography on theology and ethics. For those who desire further references, I recommend that they consult some representative academic works concerning biblical ethics and theology, for example: Ben Witherington III, *New Testament Theology and Ethics*, 2 vols. (Downers Grove, IL: InterVarsity, 2008); David P. Gushee and Glen H. Stassen, *Kingdom Ethics: Following Jesus in Contemporary Context*, 2nd ed. (Grand Rapids: Eerdmans, 2016); Robertson McQuilkin and Paul Copan, *An Introduction to Biblical Ethics: Walking in the Way of Wisdom*, 3rd ed. (Downers Grove, IL: InterVarsity, 2014); Thomas Ogletree, *The Use of the Bible in Christian Ethics* (Louisville, KY: Westminster/John Knox, 2003); Wayne Grudem, *Christian Ethics: An Introduction to Biblical Moral Reasoning* (Wheaton, IL: Crossway, 2018); and Bruce C. Birch, Jacqueline E. Lapsley, et al., *Biblical Ethics in Christian Life: A New Conversation* (Minneapolis: Fortress, 2018).

Chapter 1

Chaos

Dear Mark, Tim, and Friends:

Let's begin these letters with the basic problem of chaos and the vexing question of :

Why do chaos and disorder exist in the cosmos?

This is a haunting question that has troubled many minds. The Bible has something to say about chaos and God in its first book, Genesis. In it is contained the great story of how God sought and continues seeking to bring order out of chaos. Indeed, the Bible begins with a non-created God who not only creates, but also forms and orders a formless void into a reality (e.g. Gen. 1:1-25, Heb. 11:3) in which humans—the pinnacle of God's creation—live and experience life as they know it (Gen. 1:26-30).

The forming or the ordering of this reality has not yet been completed. It is an ongoing process because chaos has not yet been fully overcome and awaits its final consummation and ordering when the Kingdom of God will be brought to completion at the end of created time (Rev. 21:1-6). But in the meantime, creation is still ongoing (cf. Rom. 8:19-23).

On this point, I remember from my grade school days reading a book by Sir James Jeans, the royal astronomer in Britain. He said something I have never forgotten: space is expanding. Wow, I thought: that is mind-boggling! Since that time, I have come to realize the vast implications of such an idea. If space is expanding, what does that do with our concepts of cosmic permanence?

Can the Bible help us with the question of chaos?

Let's begin with the initial story of creation in the Bible that affirms the powerful acts of God, the Creator, are "very good" (Gen. 1:31). But how does that relate to chaos? That question brings us to the next or following biblical story that asserts there is an aspect within creation that remains chaotic or disruptive (Gen. 3:1-6). This chaotic aspect can be variously viewed as disharmony, evil, rebellion, sin, or opposition to the will or desires of God. Moreover, disharmony fits well into the idea of continual change.

In contrast to the stories of many other ancient religious texts, the origin of this chaotic reality such as the origin of God is not addressed in the Bible. Nevertheless, its presence can be clearly perceived within creation itself. This negative presence in the created order is variously described in terms of cosmic catastrophes or portrayed through actions of strange creatures such as the sly serpent in Genesis 3 and the powerful dragon in Revelation 12.

While such disharmony, power, and craftiness may intimidate, confuse, and lead humans to turn against their Creator, this chaotic, rebellious, destructive, anti-force in the world—epitomized in the figures of the devil, Satan, Apollyon, Abadon, etc.—is clearly understood as no match for the Creator who is defined as the Almighty—the *pantochrator* (cf. Rev. 1:8, probably the most powerful descriptor available in Greek). It is, moreover, intriguing that in the story of the defeating of the dragon in Revelation 12 that God's self does not need to dispatch or defeat the dragon. Instead, God uses the intermediacy of the archangel Michael to do the work, thus giving the reader a greater sense of the "almightiness" or power of God and the Lamb (Rev. 12:7-12).

How does the existence of both God and chaos impact humanity?

In spite of the existence of this negative reality, the almighty Creator endowed humans with a true sense of freedom that includes the ability to disobey the directives of their Creator and actually choose to promote rebellion, disorder, and chaos. This endowment of humanity means that the Almighty has to some extent limited the divine self. Nevertheless, the Bible firmly asserts that God does not abandon creation as some absentee ruler might do. God is always present, even when disorder and chaos seem to be overwhelming and when hopelessness seems to be the only option. Indeed, disorder and the evil power structure have not received absolute power to function within the created order. Ultimate power, the Bible firmly asserts, belongs only to God!

How does God respond to chaos and freedom?

When God gave a certain freedom to evil powers and humans, God also made those who receive such endowments responsible for the proper use of that freedom. All knowledgeable creatures, therefore, are accountable and must pay for the misuse of their gifts of understanding and freedom. Now even though there is natural chaos in our reality because of change, those who perpetrate additional chaos will be judged severely for causing further disruption or chaos in the universe either in time or at the *eschaton* (end of time).

Moreover, no one should be surprised that Almighty God is fully capable of using evil and disruptive forces to punish or neutralize other evil and disruptive forces that are the focus of God's punishment (see Ps. 75:2-7, Jer. 51:6-10, Ezek. 38:14-23). Clearly history testifies that many earthly malevolent and ruthless forces, which at one point proclaimed themselves to be omnipotent, soon or not so soon thereafter (in terms of time) have discovered that they were swept away by other forces proclaiming themselves to be mightier than the preceding forces they defeated. People and evil forces are not and never will be omnipotent!

How should Christians respond to freedom and chaos?

While many humans continue to espouse the fist, the sword, the cannon, the bomb, and the rocket as their symbols of security, weapons are not ultimate and can only offer temporary protection against a more devastating and powerful attack. Moreover, weapons that promise protection for their users are themselves also potentially destructive and do not prevent the dissolution and defeat of a group, a tribe, a nation, or a people from within. Placing trust in arms and armament is a futile long-range symbol of hope.

It is certainly a viable option within the context of true freedom for a person, a group, or a people to believe that God is unnecessary to the functioning of their lives or to our cosmic reality. In fact, many do so and proceed throughout life on that basis. But devotees of such a view must be prepared to accept the fact that life then has little ultimate meaning if there is no divine intention in the creation and in the ordering of reality. Still, since God provided created beings with such freedom—even to deny or disbelieve in the divine existence—we must be prepared to acknowledge their right to do so.

Yet God did not leave humans—even unbelievers—without a counter approach, and that is why God has acted repeatedly to indicate there is an option to chaos. Chaos thrives on confusion, error, lying, and hate while order thrives on truth, integrity, and love. In sending Jesus, God made it clear that wars, violence, and ill will can cease only when true love prevails or when God intervenes to terminates evil. This messenger son of God, Jesus, was the epitome of love (1 John 4:7-18, John 13:34). His self-giving death for humanity was a stark contrast to the myopic self-centeredness of people in the world who would rather fight than yield in humility to their Creator.

God, of course, could have created humans as automatons who would do his bidding like puppets, but puppets cannot freely express love to God or to other puppets. True love requires a freedom of expression, and God gave humans the freedom both to love and to hate (1 John 3:4-16). The story of the Bible is one of a loving God who created humanity to love responsibly. Instead, humans most often have chosen to focus on themselves and their well-being rather than on the loving God who helps us to love others. Notice, in this respect, that in the story of Adam and Eve their self-centeredness fractured not only their relationship with God but also with each other (Gen. 3:5-7, 12). But to understand the situation correctly, we must contrast the self-oriented statements of the humans with the actions of God who created them in love (Gen. 2:18, 20-25). And even though they were severely judged for their disobedience, God still took care of them by providing substantial covering to replace their fragile fig leaves (Gen. 3:21).

This story of Adam and Eve is far more than a mere story. It is a super-motif for the way in which God deals in love with his creation. Note also that when God chose to bless Abram/Abraham, his goal was not singular but rather long range: to bless the rest of humanity through Abraham (Gen. 12:1-3). Yet the overall story of the Bible is also the story of how humanity in the pursuit of self-centered freedom continually strays from the will of God, which inevitably leads to chaos and results in judgment and punishment.

The repeated refrain in the prophets of the Old Testament is God's mournful question: Why do the chosen people whom God loves and blesses constantly forsake their Lord, commit apostasy with other gods, practice all sorts of evil acts, and join their fortunes to other nations for security (cf. Isa. 5:8-30; Hos. 4:1-3, 6:4-6; Jer. 2:1-19; Mic. 3:9-12)? In spite of Israel's unfaithfulness, the prophets are quick to call God's people to repentance and proclaim that the loving God will yet provide a message of hope for his erring people (cf. Isa. 7:11-14; Jer. 31:1-40; Hos. 11:8-9, 14:4-9; Mic. 6:6-8, 7:18-20). That hope about which the prophets spoke was fulfilled in the coming of Jesus, God's special servant who was despised and rejected and the one on whom was placed the iniquity or guilt of everyone—because we are all sinners (Isa. 53:1-6).

It was through this Jesus that God sought to establish a new community, the church, that would be built and ordered on the basis of a dependent faith in Jesus, God's only Son; evidenced in the world by a loving relationship among its members; and destined to be driven by a powerful eschatological hope of a future life in the presence of the eternal God. These three identifying marks of a Christian are also the identifying marks of an authentic Christian community that acknowledges the superintendence of God in humans and in the ordering of the universe.

While it is sadly evident that the Christian community may not always represent the God of order and instead act as the purveyor of disorder, chaos, and even war, the church was originally chartered by Christ to be a people of a living faith who believe in the power of the Resurrection. This power-ful hinge point of Christianity is the guarantee that God is actively at work providing the divine presence in humans to counteract the failure of Adam, Eve, and their successors (1 Cor. 15:12-22). Indeed, the church's people are to be known by their self-giving love, following the model command of their master, the Lord Jesus (John 13:34-35, 15:12-17), and living in the expecta-tion of one day being gathered by the risen Lord to praise God in heaven. But in the present, they await his coming *parousia* (his final presence or return, cf. 1 Thess. 4:15-17) when sin and chaos will be vanquished and all things will finally be reconciled and ordered through Jesus (Col. 1:15-20, 1 Cor. 15:51-57).

While ultimate love, peace, and order may not be fully achievable in the present era, the Christian community has been called by Christ to approxi-mate that goal on earth. As ambassadors for the Lord, the church is expected to model for the world the intentions of God in sending Jesus to be the reconciler (2 Cor. 5:17-20) of all things both on earth and in all reality (Col. 1:19-20).

The task assigned to you, as ambassadors for Christ in the midst of chaos, may seem to be daunting. But chaos is nothing new for God. Through Christ, God has sent the Spirit (John 15:26) to assist you in this mission. And the Spirit will guide in your task of bringing integrity to the world (16:13). There-fore, trust the leading of the Spirit because it is the way of love, peace, and divinely ordained order.

Love,
Dad / Dr. B.

Questions for Reflection

- How does Dr. B. try to explain both the existence of a loving God and the presence of evil in our world? How do you try to do so?
- How do you deal with the continuing existence of chaos, wars, and deception in our world today? How do you explain chaos, conflict, and sin in your life as a Christian? How do you handle it?
- How does Dr. B. deal with the role of freedom in relation to chaos in the life of a Christian? How far does your freedom extend? Are there limits to your freedom? How does your understanding of the coming of Jesus relate to your freedom? Explain.
- Do you consider that God is a loving God? If yes, then how does such a loving God fit into your understandings of hate in the world?
- To what extent do you think it is possible to eliminate hate and chaos in the world?

Chapter 2

Equality

Dear Mark, Tim, and Friends:

We next need to address a subject that has plagued humans almost from the beginning of time:

Why are there problems of discrimination among humans?
There is a conflict innate within humans that actually sets us against ourselves. On the one hand, we struggle for an identity: we try to distinguish ourselves as positively different from others. This quest for identity means that we tend to affirm chaos by seeking to rise above the crowd. But in the process, we frequently attack or reduce the value of others to assert ourselves. Even our educational, governmental, and business systems tend to magnify those who distinguish themselves above others. On the other hand, there is a sense within us that we should seek and promote community and companionship and affirm cooperation and friendship. These two innate drives go back to a composite understanding of both the creation and the Fall in the Book of Genesis.

How does Genesis treat the two driving senses of humans?
In the initial creation story of Genesis about how God "ordered" the cosmic realm, the writer tells us that God makes humanity in the divine image as both male and female and that not only instructs them to multiply but also gives them the divinely ordained task of superintending the rest of creation (Gen 1:26-28). In the next chapter there is a slightly different description of creation in which the man is first formed but finds no satisfactory counterpart in the world, so thereafter the woman is formed from the man as a separate entity. But the two entities are related by what is usually translated as the man's "rib" (2:21-22).[1] The closeness or companionship of the two is then affirmed by reference to the fact that in their nakedness they are unashamed (2:25). Both their unity and separateness are thus positively asserted.

In the next chapters, however, because of their disobedience to God, their closeness of relationship is ruptured and the subsequent detachment is represented by the Hebrew writer in the description of how the couple sews "girdles" of fig leaves to cover their nakedness (3:7). And after portraying the tragic violation of the divine proscription related to their desire to be like God (3:4-5), the Genesis writer details the steep plunge of humanity into the chaos of fractured relationships. This negative spiral continues beyond the couple and is highlighted by the disharmony among humans (4:23-24) and even by the murder of one of the couple's offspring (4:8). As a result, within just a few pages of text after the creation account, God is grieved at having created humanity (6:5) and decides to destroy by a flood the human race—with the exception of one family (6:5-8).

How has God sought to answer the human dilemma?

The sad story of humanity then becomes a repeated refrain of God's grace in needing to start over the human process because scarcely is the family of Noah out of the ark when new violations occur (Gen. 9:20-25). So, God turns to Abraham and the formation of a covenant community that will be a blessing "to all the families of the earth" (12:1-3). But the Old Testament is the sad record of God trying repeatedly to develop a committed, community-oriented, obedient people who will be faithful to God and who will treat others including foreigners—not just Israelites/Jews—with loving care. Stories such as that of Jonah remind us that God wants to reach out beyond this covenant community, but the response is hardly a positive one (Jonah 4:1-5, 9-11).

How has Jesus impacted the story of human community?

God finally sends his own son to portray for humanity what loving, self-giving humility and caring obedience is like. But the covenant community rejects God's agent and with their Roman conquerors kill God's model. Yet that divine-human model also becomes the saving and transforming means to achieve a new authenticity (salvation) and to establish a new community that is intended to be a genuine pattern for the world of what acceptance should be without making unloving and divisive distinctions. Love is to be the key to a God-honoring community (John 13:34-35, 15:12).

Has the pattern set by Jesus worked?

Obviously, the pattern set by Jesus has not worked very consistently! The story of Peter and Cornelius in Acts 10, however, is a great example of the ideal intention and should be a vivid challenge to the Christian community of what acceptance should be like.

Cornelius, a Gentile Roman—who has sought to be a caring, praying non-Jew from the great city of Caesarea—is informed by the Lord to seek the assistance of Peter for spiritual direction. In the same story, Peter—who tries to be an observant Jew—is challenged three times by the Lord not to reject non-kosher food that the Lord has cleansed. When the agents of Cornelius arrive at Joppa where Peter is staying, Peter recognizes that the Spirit is challenging him to accept a new perspective and so he invites the Gentiles into the Jewish home (10:23).

Then going with the Gentiles to the home of Cornelius, Peter admits to them that God is "not partial" and thus shares the gospel with the Gentiles (10:34-43). To the surprise of the Jewish believers, God actually confirms Peter's proclamation of "no distinction" by sending the Holy Spirit to the Gentiles (10:44-46). With such a confirmation from God, Peter has no option but to baptize them and affirm that they are accepted as followers of Jesus (10:47-48). But news of the incident quickly reaches the Jewish believers in Jerusalem, and some are very disturbed. Naturally, Peter is called to defend his actions. For the sake of the Christian church, when those critics hear Peter's explanation, they are silenced. At this point the believers recognize that God is doing something new in their midst and that the Jewish-Gentile distinction should no longer be regarded as legitimate (11:16-18).

The issue is not fully resolved, however. It festers among a segment of the church called the circumcision party, and Paul has to tackle the subject later with none other than Peter/Cephas over the issue of Jewish Christians eating with Gentiles at Antioch. Fortunately, for the church the apostolic fire-brand, Paul, stands firm in his convictions concerning justification by faith and will not yield to Peter's waffling (cf. Gal. 2:11-21). Accordingly, the fiercely logical argument that Paul develops in Galatians as a result serves as the foundation for the strategic resolution of the Gentile inclusion in the church at the Jerusalem Council in Acts 15.[2] Moreover, the Pauline proclamation that "There is no longer Jew or Greek/Gentile, slave or free, male and female because you are all one in Christ Jesus" has become the great Christian summons to equality for all people (Gal. 3:28).

But do Christians really believe people are created equal?

Most people in the United States are familiar with Martin Luther King Jr. and his great dream for America to be free from segregation and how he was assassinated in 1968 for advocating that dream. We also know about the 2017 tragedy that took place in Charlottesville, Virginia, in connection with those who marched for maintaining the monuments of the men who led the cause of separation in America, burned torches, and stood for their ideas of white supremacy. And I could enumerate countless other incidents in the recent history of the U.S. that indicate a lack of equality in this country—and throughout the world.

Many people on earth are radically divided on issues related to people being created equal in the sight of God. We humans seem to focus on divisions and differences rather than on unity and harmony—and Christians seem to choose that route as well. We may mouth our commitments to community and equality, but the model of love that Jesus gave us in the Christian imperative seems to be a hard message for his followers to accept. Rather than detailing here the repeated failures of Christians to adopt the command of Jesus to "love one another" and to follow the proclamation of Paul concerning "no distinctions," I would ask you to ponder the following experience.

This experience did not make the headlines in our newspapers nor summon television crews to descend on a particular site to capture the latest facts on tape for the evening news. But this situation was very real and may raise the eyebrows of some who have been in the forefront of the Civil Rights Movement and of the goal of furthering equal rights for all people.

It took place a few years ago when I was the dean of Northern Seminary in the Chicago area. One of our superb African-American women students asked me if I would preach the sermon for her ordination service in an African-American church in downtown Chicago. She told me she wanted her friends in the inner city to understand the implications of ordination for her. I readily agreed to the student's request not only because I enjoy preaching in African-American churches where there are great responses between the preacher and the people, but also because I thought this woman was a genuinely authentic representative of her community and of Christ. Yet when her pastor extended the invitation for African-American clergy to join in reviewing her and in the service itself, he received a series of resounding refusals from his colleagues because the ordination was of a woman!

When I heard about this response of the African-American brotherhood, I began to ask myself some penetrating questions about how we as Christians use the Bible. Do we in the church use the well-known biblical text from Galatians 3:28 about no distinctions between Jews and Greeks, slave and free, male and female selectively when it suits our purposes but then reject its relevance when it does not fit our views? Here was a group of very vocal ministers who had repeatedly quoted this text from Galatians to advance their civil rights goals yet who refused to acknowledge the significance of the same text when it came to their presuppositions concerning women in ministry.

I began to wonder: Is this pattern a common practice among Christians? Do we happily use the Bible when we find it useful but avoid its message when it threatens our presuppositions? The more I thought about that question, the more concerned I became for the integrity of Christian proclamation. Lack of integrity visits the church quite frequently.

But on this issue of equality it is particularly problematic because the New Testament and particularly the Apostle Paul seem to be convinced that in sending Jesus, God was making no distinctions in us as sinners and in receiving God's grace (Rom. 3:22, 10:12). So, we need to ask ourselves in all seriousness: What does it really mean when Paul said that "we are all one in Christ Jesus" (Gal. 3:28)? The world loves to make distinctions, but I fear that we in the church are also still learning what this verse implies. Mouthing words of accepting the Scripture as the inspired word of God does not mean that we also accept the implications of those words.

How would you have responded to this discrimination against a female by male clergy?

I must admit that I was very saddened not only because of these ministers' selective use of the Bible, but also because they rejected one of their own preachers who modeled the best in relating the Bible to the needs of people. Today, of course, such a situation would probably engender a huge series of tweeted responses such as "#MeToo." But those brothers, I am sure, thought they were "on the side of God," little realizing that God would later use this young woman and her preaching to bless people, especially among the African Americans in the Chicago area and beyond. The women and all people in our churches need our support because God wants and needs everyone's witness to the world.

What then should we say about issues of submission and Christian relationships?

The issue of submission engenders a great deal of hostility among people. Indeed, among Christians it involves misunderstandings in the interpretation of several important biblical texts concerning family relationships. Remember that in the Roman world during the time of Jesus, the caesar regarded his empire as his family whom he controlled. The emperor was viewed as a father who gave rules that his subjects had to obey as though they were his children. We call the concept that emerged the family or "household" codes. When we compare the ancient household codes to the New Testament codes, we note that there were no rules in the ancient family codes for husbands, fathers, and masters. They made the rules, and the rules applied to wives, children, and slaves!

The New Testament writers were very familiar with the household codes and used the concept to explain relationships in the Christian community. While partial codes are included in the Pastoral Letters, the most obvious ones are found in Colossians 3:18–4:1 and in 1 Peter 3:1-7. The most complete "Christian code" in the New Testament, however, is recorded in Ephesians 5:21–6:9. Notice how that code begins: "Be subject/submissive to one another out of reverence for Christ." In other words, everything one does is *in response* to the "caesarship" or lordship of Christ (5:21)! What follows then is that wives are naturally expected to recognize the lordship of their husbands. This idea was hardly new within either Judaism or the Hellenistic world.

But in this text the lordship idea is viewed more as an "under-lordship" for the husbands because it is patterned on the relationship of Christ and the church (5:22-23). Notice, however, that husbands are not to regard themselves as rulers in the marriage relationship but are to adopt the servant model of Jesus who "gave himself" for the church (5:25; cf. John 13). I have been intrigued in reading interpretations of this statement by how many writers seem to avoid saying what "gave himself" actually means. It means Jesus "died" for us!

I repeatedly have asked my students: What does a relationship look like when a husband actually sacrifices everything about himself, including his life, for his wife? I think this is a very different kind of relationship than that which is usually evidenced in our society—and even in many Christian families. Perhaps that is the reason there is so much attention being given currently to the quest among women for recognition—even in the church. I do not think that we as Christian clergy and laity have taken with sufficient seriousness in the church the summons to equality of submission under Christ and the identity of women.

But this comment leads me to an intriguing observation concerning the text in 1 Peter. After an elongated statement about Christian women being submissive to their non-Christian husbands in order to win them to Jesus (1 Pet. 3:1-6), the writer turns to Christian men and almost shocks them with a reminder about how they are to treat their Christian wives—as "joint heirs" of God's gracious gift of new life. But then the writer flashes a big stick at the men in case they are not paying attention, adding "in order that your prayers may not be short-circuited" (3:7). In other words, if you don't treat your wives like Christ would, don't expect God to listen to your prayers! This statement is a straightforward warning to men. (I have a feeling that this text is not mentioned in many Christian men's meetings!)

What about the father-child relationship? Of course, children are expected to be obedient and honor their parents (Eph. 6:1-2). This message is nothing new. In fact, it is the first commandment with a promise and is encapsulated in the Decalogue (#5; Exod. 20:12, Deut. 5:16). While the Jewish tradition regarded children as a blessing, in the Hellenistic world children were not always so regarded. Stories of domineering and cruel fathers were not unknown, and unwanted babies were periodically even left exposed to the elements. But what is crucial in this text is that fathers are warned that, like Abraham, they have a God-given responsibility or duty of disciplining and instructing their children in the ways of the Lord *without* provoking them to rebel (6:4).

What about the master-slave relationship? Naturally, slaves are expected to be obedient. Such is nothing new, but as Christians their obedience should not be merely because they fear punishment or desire reward. They are to do so because they are servants of Christ (Eph. 6:5-6). But masters are forcefully warned to avoid threatening slaves because they as masters are subject to their ultimate Master—and that "Master in heaven does not make distinctions" (6:9). Do you understand the radical nature of that statement? Without much fanfare, for Christianity, the end of slavery is on the horizon! It is similar to the statement in Philemon when Paul tells his friend to treat Onesimus "no longer as a slave but as a beloved brother" (Phlm. 16).

Do you see how the equality of people is especially important in family life? And if it applies to the family, it will ultimately touch all human relationships. Yet I fear that we tend to read the New Testament texts as though they are simply a rehash of old Hellenistic views. But the coming of Christ made a radical difference in the way people are expected to relate to one another.

What is your thinking on texts about the women's testimonies related to Jesus and about Simon of Cyrene?

As I have traveled around the world, I have collected pictures of Jesus and—as you might guess—those pictures are not all of a white man and do not all show Jesus with long brown hair. Some pictures and etchings in the early catacombs and ancient churches depict Jesus with short hair. The long hair depiction probably arose in the minds of artists because of the confusion or merging of Nazarene (from Nazareth) and Nazarite (a consecrated Israelite). This fact concerning perspectives has led me to ponder a number of other questions about how we interpret our ancient biblical texts.

Some contemporary people have supposed that Simon of Cyrene who carried Jesus' cross (cf. Mark 15:21, Matt. 27:32, Luke 23:26) was a black man—because he came from North Africa (in Libya). Yet, Cyrene was a Roman city founded by Dorian Greeks that lay 100 miles west of modern Benghazi. Simon's sons, Alexander and Rufus, definitely have Hellenistic names. So how do we imagine who Simon was? Why do you think the Romans conscripted him?

Then, have you ever asked yourself about the women's testimonies concerning the resurrection of Jesus in the Gospels? Were women's testimonies important to the ancients? If they were not too significant, would that perspective have something to do with the way the biblical writers deal with their testimonies? Remember: after the death of Jesus, the risen Lord appeared first to women (Matt. 28:9-10, John 20:14-18)! I do not think that this phenomenon is a matter of inspiration, but perhaps more of our human perception and our time-bound perspectives. We must be careful in the way we interpret the Scriptures.

Because I take the Bible very seriously, let me pursue this matter further. The above comments lead me to remind you of the fascinating statement in the Gospel of Mark concerning the anointing of Jesus in Bethany. After the anointing, Jesus said to his bewildered disciples something intriguing concerning the future: "Truthfully, I tell you that wherever the gospel is preached in the whole world, what she has done will be discussed as a memorial to her" (Mark 14:9). What do you think of this statement as an affirmation of a woman's action? It certainly was futuristic! Could it be pointing to a new perspective? Could a woman be leading the followers of Jesus to a new understanding of service and worship? As you contemplate your answer, remember that the first humans to worship the risen Christ were women. And do not forget the important Hebrew exclamation of Mary when she recognized the risen Lord at the tomb: "*Rabboni!*"—"my exalted teacher!" (John 20:16). For a first-century Jew, that statement was a very lofty acclamation. Do not dismiss it lightly!

So, do you not wonder just a bit that if the resurrection of Jesus would happen today whether women and people who are not like us might receive a little more attention? What I am asking you to ponder is whether we are recognizing the continuing unveiling of truth in our midst. I like to think about how God is continuing to bring order out of the chaos that is all around us. And I firmly believe that God continues to open our minds to the greater ramifications of having sent Jesus to lead us in understanding what equality should mean for our generation.

Perhaps someday we may understand more clearly what the statement "we are all one in Christ Jesus" (Gal. 3:28) really means. Are you willing to work for a greater acceptance of equality among all people? This is a burning question for which, I believe, Christians will be called to give an accounting. Do not think for a moment that God is uninterested in our responses. Take seriously the fact that God through Christ is still acting in the midst of our chaos.

In Christ,
Dad /Dr. B.

Questions for Reflection

• Why do you think Dr. B. considers that discrimination is deep seated and reflects innate problems within humans?

• Do you think that equality among humans is possible? Why or why not?

• What kinds of patterns of discrimination do you recognize in society? At your workplace or school? In your Christian community? In your home? In yourself?

• Do you think government legislation can impact discrimination? If so, how?

• Do you think Christians can impact discrimination in your community? In our nation? If so, how?

• How did you react to Dr. B's discussion on the submission texts? Does his interpretation of the household codes help to clarify for you the meaning of those texts?

Notes

[1]There is a good deal of debate among some biblical scholars today who think there might be sexual implications in Genesis 2:21-22. I would simply note that the Hebrew can be broadly interpreted in reference to a "side" and with respect to the human body generally refers to "rib."

[2]See my argument in "Galatians" in Roger Mohrlang and Gerald L. Borchert, *Romans and Galatians*, vol. 14, Cornerstone Biblical Commentary (Carol Stream, IL: Tyndale House, 2007), especially 248-251.

Chapter 3

Integrity

Dear Mark, Tim, and Friends:

Since I mentioned integrity in reflecting on the last issue, I think it would be strategic to turn to that question immediately.

Why is integrity important to the Christian witness?

Scarcely is there a more critical issue than integrity for Christians and for all humans on Planet Earth. Yet integrity is sacrificed daily in the quest for money, power, prestige, self-enhancement, and self-defense. What I am writing to you in this message grows out of countless encounters with less than Christlike behavior by those who claim to be followers of Jesus. While I have been disturbed by some of the situations in Christian communities I have encountered, I am purposely limiting the examples I have included here and am refraining completely from making a full identification of the persons involved, even though I know well who they are. The reason is because such patterns of behavior could be duplicated in others and could easily involve any of us if we are not careful in our actions.

The lack of integrity in our society is so prevalent that we all must be careful lest we succumb to this temptation. But failure to address this question in one of the early set of questions would be inexcusable on my part. So I begin by reminding you that not only is the lack of integrity well documented in the politics of our country, but also it is unfortunately becoming more evident in the church and among Christians. Therefore, we who attempt to represent Christ and his integrity to the world are duty-bound to be reminded of our calling to live and act authentically before others. So, the next question is this:

What is the purpose of oaths?

It was because of the pervasiveness of inauthentic religious people in his day that Jesus addressed the subject of oaths. Originally, oaths were used because people did not trust others to be honest. Jesus knew that for many people "yes" did not really mean "yes," and the same was true for "no." Therefore, the rabbis and others developed oaths to assure the truthfulness of pledges, promises, and testimonies. Swearing by that which was greater than one's self was intended to assure the recipient of an oath that the promise made would be kept. But Jesus knew that humans were deceptive, so he instructed his hearers to avoid swearing by anything—e.g., not by heaven, nor by earth, nor even by one's own head—because none of those items would guarantee that a sinful person would be honest.

Indeed, the rabbis developed levels of accountability in their swearing so that if people swore by the temple, it was not a genuine commitment. But if they swore by the gold of the temple, it was absolutely binding (Matt. 23:17). Actually, Jesus understood that employing oaths was a practice clearly rooted in human perversity and manipulation (Matt. 5:33-37). He also knew that the rabbis developed clever traditions such as Corban[1] to circumvent divinely inspired patterns in caring honestly for parents and those in need (Mark 7:9-13).

The human tendency toward lying is also the reason our British and American court systems expect those who give testimonies to swear before they speak that they will tell "the truth, the whole truth, and nothing but the truth!" Unfortunately, truth-telling is not a virtue commonly present among people. Many in our world do not plan to tell the truth or keep the promises they make. They actually intend to fudge on the truth before they begin.

But the lack of integrity goes beyond truth-telling to all of our activities and relationships in life. It is precisely because of the sinful human disposition to twist not only the truth but also how we relate to one another that Jesus told his hearers: If an eye is offensive, pluck it out. If a hand offends, cut it off. It would be better to be deformed than to have one's whole being consigned to hell or to a shadowy place such as a spiritual no-man's land (Matt. 5:29-30, Mark 9:47). But our problem is that we generally do not believe that Jesus could be that serious about the Kingdom of God and "casting a person into a hellish afterlife."[2] So, we continue to play our games of manipulation with truth and relationships. Then, if and ultimately when our manipulations or untruths are discovered—as in the case of Adam and Eve in the creation story (Gen. 3:8-13)—we try to hide or, failing that course of action, we turn to blaming others for our terrible state of affairs.

Furthermore, in the stories of the temptation of Jesus we are reminded that the devil is fully capable of quoting Scripture and manipulating it to serve the purposes of evil (Matt. 4:1-11, Luke 4:1-13). Do not be surprised that it is quite possible for those who espouse the Christian name to feel justified in using the Bible for selfish and evil purposes. If the devil tried to do it with Jesus, he is fully capable of confusing people to do the same so that they act like the devil. For example, I have witnessed multiple times when preachers who staunchly proclaim the importance of "love" at one point in their sermons turn and employ deceit, fear, and hate in another segment of their messages—all in the name of Jesus! So, be very careful that you do not fall into that trap of confused devilish practices and motives.

And this statement brings me to another question:

What are some examples of the lack of integrity?

Perhaps the following brief illustration might be helpful at this point. It involved a very bright young man who wanted to gain stature in his faith community. After a major meeting of his denomination, he reached the realization that the perspectives he was promoting in his work were not popular with his constituency. He thereupon declared to others that they were on the wrong side and needed to change sides if they were to gain a hearing and become popular with the people. He promptly did so and was quickly recognized by his new side as a hero. Accordingly, it did not take long for him to gain public attention and status among his new side.

Now this story may not seem to be unusual in a world of politics but while the church is a political reality, the question that confronts us becomes: What is the church's primary focus? And we might also ask: In the light of Paul's description of Christ as a servant model (Phil. 2:1-11), what concern if any should Christians have in doing whatever they can to seek higher political, social, and church positions even if it means manipulation, lying, and changing one's orientations?

I could at this point detail many other manipulative moves taken by leaders in the pursuit of their careers, but that is unnecessary if we ask the fundamental question Pilate asked Jesus: "What is truth?" (John 18:38). I suspect that for a politician, truth is a convenient tool to use and manipulate for the purposes of political advantage. But, of course, in such a framework the whole truth is unnecessary. Yet some truth is essential for the political goal not to appear to be questionable and shrouded in doubt. For example, we can attempt to hide our previous statements that would appear to be contrary to political or theological positions that must be taken if we are to advance in our new position or recently changed status. But that does not mean we cannot change our mind on matters. We all do that in our growing understanding of issues—as long as we can freely admit to a change of perspectives.

The point in such misleading practices, of course, is that the end justifies the means. But the Christian response must be that if unjust or dishonest means are used to attain a desired goal, then the resulting goal is actually encrusted with injustice and dishonesty. In such a mixed pattern of life a just or honest goal will never be attained because it is skewed from the outset. While politicians may answer that such a sacrifice is necessary to obtain even a partial goal, in the church such a sacrifice impairs the integrity of the Christian message of truth and can only be severely condemned as inauthentic and actually evil.

Concerning another leader, I learned the sad story from a person who was seeking a higher position in his denomination but was told in no uncertain terms that he was not yet ready. When he inquired why not, the response was so toxic that I cannot repeat it. But I would merely say that to expect a Christian to hurt other Christians in order to acquire a higher position of leadership in the church or denomination is a total denial of Christ's message to the world.

When I was in seminary and graduate school, I read a number of books detailing how some ancient and medieval leaders had acted on behalf of the church. I was absolutely embarrassed for the sake of Jesus and the gospel. But I have since discovered that some leaders in my own denomination have been just as embarrassing to the name of Jesus and the gospel. My sons and dear friends, for the sake of our Savior, Jesus, turn your back and flee even the thought of using misleading and evil practices in the church.

But this conclusion leads to a further question:

How should Christians respond to the lack of integrity?

This question reminds me of something that my wise pastor back in Canada told me as I was preparing to leave for seminary and study for the ministry. He said, "Jerry, I want you always to remember that truth wears no labels. It is neither liberal nor conservative. Truth is truth. I want you to promise me that you will commit yourself to the truth."

That statement contained some of the best advice I have received in ministry. Since that time, I have taught in places considered by others to be either liberal or conservative. But like all authentic Christian and non-Christian teachers, I have tried to make it my goal to teach the truth as best as I can and not pin labels on other people. So, I would charge all of us: "Always aim for the truth." And for Christians I would add: "Aim for the truth in Jesus," because the truth that is in Jesus will never be false or evil. Moreover, the truth that is in Jesus is wonderfully freeing and will always seek the best for others. To live for Jesus and the truth is to discover genuine freedom (John 8:32).

Truth and deception are polar opposites. And as Jesus indicated, deception and lying are from the devil who was a liar from the beginning (John 8:43-44). But integrity was embodied in Jesus—the unique person who was in fact the *way* to God, the portrait of *truth* and the reality of *life* (John 14:6).

Manipulation and lying are very successful tools of the devil. They are quite at home in the world, but also frequently visit churches. Indeed, church business meetings are great settings for manipulation and for the presence of the devil, especially when tools such as *Robert's Rules of Order* are used to silence minority opinions. Of course, rules are needed to get things done, but we must never forget that majorities are not always right! So, another question then confronts us:

If a minority can sometimes be right/correct, how does a Christian majority deal with a minority?

This question forces us to face the reality that whatever pattern of church polity we use or how many persons are involved in the decision-making process, we may not always be Christlike in our conduct. We may in fact be more interested in winning—and winning at the earliest stage possible, so as not to risk the opportunity for our view to fail. To pass motions and arrive at decisions we want or to achieve the goals we seek often become for us more important than the advancement of Christlike conduct and relationships. Allowing opportunity to ponder alternative views is difficult for humans. Yet it often takes time to arrive at Christlike answers. We usually know the Christlike way because it cares about the people involved just as much and perhaps more than getting the decision made. The pattern of caring for the people involved in a process is one of the greatest lessons we all have to learn in order to attain Christlike decisions.

In business meetings and in dealing with activities, resources, and properties of the church, Christians can often become quite devil-like. I would suggest that we ponder the reasons why such might be the case. It might be revealing to reflect on just how invested we can become in business matters.

Can Christians fit into Jesus' harsh criticisms of the Pharisees?

Remember: Jesus condemned the Pharisees because they neglected the weightier matters of the law—"justice, mercy, and faith" (Matt. 23:23). They did not like that evaluation. What about us?

In reflecting on this question, let me choose an illustration that will not touch us in North America. This concern for property and other business matters reminds me of the time I was living in Israel and observed the actions of two priests from the communions in charge of the Church of the Holy Sepulcher. It was Palm Sunday morning, and they were screaming at each other! They nearly became engaged in an intense physical fight over their time for control of the tomb in order to collect donations from pilgrims and visitors to this historic site. As I watched in wonderment, the startling thought crossed my mind: They are fighting over the tomb of Jesus—who is *not* there! Is that not a fascinating commentary?

But to carry the illustration further, I am also reminded of the fact that the various communions in that historic church have an amazing inability to agree on anything. For example, all the groups in charge of that building must agree to make any changes. But since they could not agree on the badly needed renovations, it continued to deteriorate to the point of being a hazard for the thousands of pilgrims who visit the site regularly. Finally, the Israeli government stepped into the situation and threatened to close the structure if the groups in the church could not agree to make repairs. That threat of losing donations from tourists, however, quickly brought the groups together and now the site is being repaired. But visitors to the church will also notice as they enter the church that there is a ladder propped up against the outside wall on the upper level of the church. Many years ago it was left by an attendant in error, but it remains standing there and has become a silent symbol of the dysfunctional self-centeredness and outright hostility that exist among the church leaders there. They cannot even remove the ladder until all agree that it should be done! Do you think the Jews and Muslims in Jerusalem are unaware of the pettiness of the Christians there?

How should we evaluate current practices of church order?

Given the nature of humanity and the goal of Christianity to model the way of integrity with Jesus, I often remind my students that the church is not called to be a democracy. And I doubt that it should be an autocracy or a dictatorship. I think it would be better understood as a *pnuematocracy* (the rule of

のOFF

OFF

the Spirit). Yet, getting a community of believers to be centered on the Spirit and on God is a challenge for "me-centered," narcissistic humans.

Nevertheless, I believe that is what God hoped the early church would become and what I think is being attempted in the early chapters of the Book of Acts. But it has been difficult for Christians to follow the leading of the Spirit. We want to lead, but to lead authentically we need the guidance of God's Spirit. With the Spirit directing our path, we can become authentic leaders. Without the Spirit, Christians are like willow branches bending with the changing winds.

What are our goals as Christians in terms of integrity?

Briefly let me refer to another example that relates to Christian integrity. One of my bright doctoral students informed me that he was going to the church convention and would visit with one of the two leaders who were determined to reshape the denomination in which we belonged. When he came back to the seminary after the visit, I did not want to infringe on his goals but I suggested that he should take care and weigh carefully his meeting and any advice given. But above all, I asked him to commit himself to integrity as a Christian. I am not sure whether he remembered my words, but they may have been displaced as he gained stature in the denomination.

We drifted apart as I left that seminary to teach elsewhere but his son, who had grown up with the desire to make sure he was absolutely prepared for heaven, soon attended the seminary and became an exceedingly bright and forceful Christian writer. He moved to New York where he encountered many people who were completely unfamiliar with what he calls "Christianese"—the insider language of Christians particularly in the South. Thankfully, the son's wrestling with himself and his integrity did not drive him away from God as it has done with a number of other young people in our era who have seen the sham in some Christians and their "God talk." Instead, I am grateful that God has called this son to summon others to "speak God" authentically in ways that people will again recognize the incredible nature of what God has done in Christ for humanity. I am also grateful that he and his dad have a good relationship, which is not always true of our younger generation with their parents.

Jesus understood the nature of authenticity and what it was not. He advised his followers *not* to practice their piety before people to gain their approval. They were not to be like those who wished they could sound a bugle before they made a significant donation to the temple (something akin to the loud clanging that took place when people dumped a large number of coins into the metal treasury bins in the temple; cf. Matt. 6:2-4). And they were not to be like those who stood on street corners and recited their long religious prayers where everyone around could see and hear their pious actions (Matt. 6:5). God is quite familiar with why and how we practice our piety, and the Lord is not impressed with showmanship.

Perhaps among the early followers of Jesus the Apostle Paul understood this message of pseudo-piety most clearly because he had been a Pharisee—a member of the group that received the scathing rebukes of Jesus as detailed in Matthew 23. After his encounter with Jesus in his letters, the Christian Saul/Paul gives a great deal of attention in his letters to the integrity of Christians in both worship and life. Religious showmanship is for him a betrayal of true faith in Christ. That is the reason he sternly rejects the outward practices of the Galatians (Gal. 6:12), but calls them instead to produce the results of God's Spirit in them—love, joy, peace, patience, kindness, goodness, faithfulness, gentleness, and self-control (Gal. 5:22). Similarly, he instructs the Romans to let their "love be genuine" (Rom. 12:9), "to contribute to the poor," to "bless those who persecute you," and to "live in harmony with one another" (12:14-16). Likewise, he challenges his Corinthian misfits to "examine" themselves and "test" their lives to find out whether their faith in Jesus Christ is authentic. Will they pass that test (2 Cor. 13:5-6)? Maybe that question should be directed to us, too.

To the same end, Paul exhorts Timothy, his son in the faith, that he should remind Christians to "avoid disputing about words … [and all such] non-productive chatter" (2 Tim. 2:14). In addition, he warns his younger companion about associating with those who merely have a form of religion but lack its authority and power (2 Tim. 3:5). Then, to Titus, Paul sums up his goal for Christian leadership as being "a model of doing good deeds" and of demonstrating in teaching the qualities of "integrity, seriousness, and soundness of ideas" so that his views might not be dismissed as lacking in authenticity and significance (Titus 2:7).

These words of advice from the great apostle still have the ring of truth two millennia after they were written. They are worthy of adoption today. Therefore, my sons and readers, as you engage in your various ministries and service for Christ, I pray that you will not fail in the test of authenticity. Truth is truth. The world does not think that truth is important. But for Jesus, truth was the measuring standard of life. Sacrificing truth puts a person in the camp of the devil. For the sake of Christ and the gospel: commit yourself to the truth!

Love,
Dad/Dr. B.

Questions for Reflection

- How would you define integrity? Why do you think Dr. B. considers integrity to be such an important issue for Christians?
- How important do you think integrity is for Christians? Have you encountered Christians who lack integrity? What has been your reaction to them? Do you think they hinder the message of the gospel? If so, how?
- What do you think it means for Jesus to be "the way, the truth, and the life"?
- In church business meetings, do you think a majority can deal authentically with a differing minority? Is it possible to be authentic and still disagree? Explain.
- In what ways can we understand the biblical idea of practicing one's piety before others in today's culture? How can we best avoid such practices?

Note

[1] In Jewish legal tradition, *qorban* (Hebrew) was something dedicated to God though not actually offered to God.

Chapter 4

The Battles
Christians Fight

Dear Mark, Tim, and Friends:

Having considered the importance of truth and integrity in the last chapter, it is time to approach the uncomfortable issue of the battles into which Christians are engaged.

What is behind the battles Christians are fighting, and why?[1]

One of Satan's best ways to nullify the effectiveness of the church's role in evangelizing the world for Christ is to promote internal battles within the church. These battles are quite effective because they cause chaos and shift the church's focus from its external task—namely, its mission—to an internal one, which is self-preservation!

Moreover, these battles open churches—particularly those that are more congregational in nature—to a hostile takeover by persons who employ chaos and prefer to lead by dictatorship rather than the consent of the community. When Jesus instructed Christians to take up the cross, he was commissioning them to abandon their self-concerns and be ready to die for the Lord (Matt. 16:24-27). Unfortunately, most Christians in the Western world seem more prepared to fight one another than to die for Christ. Indeed, while Christ called us to be peacemakers as blessed children of God (Matt. 5:9), Satan encourages us to be dogma-keepers who deny brotherhood and sisterhood to other Christians.

In the process of fighting, the devil leads us to focus not on just one issue but constantly moves our attention from one subject to another so that both the devil and Christians do not become bored with their battles. The devil despises peace and will do anything to manufacture frustration, upheaval, and chaos. On the other hand, love and community-building are Christ's goal for the church and for all Christians. But love is completely antithetical to the purposes of the devil. Remember: Jesus did not say that everyone would know that we are Christ's disciples by our faithfulness to dogma or fighting to defend our perspectives on our doctrine and what we think is truth. No! He insisted that people would recognize who we are by our love (John 13:35).

As far as the devil is concerned, it doesn't matter why Christians are fighting or what issue is involved. It can be anything, for example: church membership, baptism, divorce, homosexuality, the millennium, church unity, gifts of the Spirit, salvation, the Trinity, the nature of Jesus, the role of faith, tithing, the importance of good works, or the Bible. It does not matter to the devil! As long as Christians are fighting, they are not focused on following Jesus and doing God's will. And they are certainly not concentrating directly on resisting the wiles of the devil. So as far as the devil is concerned, the more battles the better! And for the devil, the "Battle for the Bible" is one of the most significant wars because the more humans argue about Scripture, the less time they have to read it. The more they use its texts for fighting, the less they can use its texts for living.

How does understanding the Pharisees and Sadducees assist us with the nuances of terms such as liberal and conservative?

So, while a good deal of attention has been given to the "Battle(s) for the Bible" in the church of the twentieth and twenty-first centuries, there were preliminary skirmishes in the eighteenth and nineteenth centuries. Yet much earlier there was an outright confrontation over interpreting Scripture between the Pharisees and Sadducees for about a century before Jesus—God's incarnate Son—came on the scene. The Jews at that time had the familiar conservative-liberal sides but, as Louis Finkelstein has indicated in his excellent work on the Pharisees, the distinctions were more nuanced.[2]

The Sadducees were theologically conservative, but in relation to the Romans they were more liberal or progressive; the Pharisees were theologically more open and progressive but politically less cooperative with the Romans and more conservative. I mention these distinctions because, to make sense of the terms "liberal" and "conservative," we must understand them not merely in their religious and theological contexts but also in their political, sociological, and cultural frameworks. Clarity in contexts is crucial. Remember that people who pride themselves on being in one camp may actually be in the opposite camp in terms of other dimensions of life.

How did Jesus and early Christians relate to disputes between the Pharisees and Sadducees?

When Jesus came to the attention of the Jewish establishment, both groups soon joined forces against him because he did not focus on disputing about the interpretation of words. Instead, his concern was about the more fundamental issue of living with God. Eschewing the knit-picking disputes of those religious leaders, Jesus called on everyone to obey or walk with God directly, not merely argue about the implications of the 613 *halakic* rules that the rabbis had isolated from the Torah. So uncomfortable with Jesus did these religious leaders become, they quickly determined that he had to be eliminated or their precious laws, traditions, and temple would not survive the call of Jesus for a direct relationship of people walking with God (see Matt 26:61; cf. the condemnation of Stephen in Acts 6:13-14). So, with the assistance of the Herodians and the Romans, this Jesus—God's personal envoy—was dispatched by means of an ugly crucifixion.

This emphasis of Jesus on a direct relationship with God—namely, walking with God—placed Jesus and his early followers in a direct confrontation or battle with the legalistic Jewish leadership. The model of walking with God provides for us, Jesus' later followers, a significant insight into the kind of battles that are worthy of Christians as over against the legalistic wranglings that are often evidenced in church and denominational circles. (For a brief review of "Walking with God," see page 40)

To the distress of the religious leaders, the death of Jesus and his subsequent resurrection greatly empowered his small group of despised, so-called non-religious folk, the *am haeretz* (people of the land)—the despised fishermen and tax-collector types who had earlier followed him. They began to proclaim him and the power of his resurrection with an amazing vigor. Indeed, from the point of view of the religious leaders, these nobodies (see 1 Cor. 1:26) were audacious in preaching about the saving power of God "in the name of this Jesus" (cf. for example Acts 3:16; 4:7, 17, 30, etc.). And even though they were warned, beaten, and threatened with death, they continued to preach about new life through Jesus. In doing so they virtually made the theological formulas and scriptural interpretations of the rabbis irrelevant, unnecessary, and passé.

If that was not enough, to distress the Great Council (the Jewish Sanhedrin), these peasants were soon joined by the brilliant Saul/Paul who had come out of Tarsus—one of the leading cities of Stoicism—and who had been sent

An Excursus on "Walking with God"

This idea of walking with God may appear to the outsider as living with a set of rules, yet it focuses not on rules but on a relationship with God. It may seem like a subjective model, but its goal is to live closely with the Spirit of God and to be directed by that Spirit, bearing in mind that Jesus gave a pattern for living to his followers while he was here on earth. That model was introduced in the Old Testament in its pre-Christian form with people who were judged acceptable—such as Enoch, Abraham, and Hezekiah—and it was even suggested in the opening chapters of Genesis when God desired to "walk" with Adam and his wife, but instead these humans tried to hide because they had ruptured their relationship with God (Gen. 3:8-10). The concept of walking with God does not attribute to humans a divine nature, but it posits a compatibility between God and humans as Amos suggested in his question: "Can two not walk together unless they agree?" (Amos 3:3).

This biblical concept of "walking" (the Hebrew verb is *halak*) with God implies a relationship between the parties, but the concept was unfortunately altered by the rabbis when they used the Hebrew noun *halakah* instead of the verb and focused on the way one walks—a set of prescriptions or rules for being acceptable to God. Then, 613 rules were identified in the Torah (the Law, the first five books of the Hebrew canon) and designated as the basic principles for obedience to God. The problem, however, is that while rules may serve as a convenient pattern for defining morality, they can be harsh and may give way to actions that in given situations could be opposed to the will of God. Our living God relates to people with loving kindness or gentle mercy (the Hebrew term is *chesed*). Apart from the issue of his identity, many of the face-offs between Jesus and the Jewish leadership involved the way both parties reached their understandings of the will of God and the ways humans conducted their lives.

It is precisely at the point of the weakness of rules, law, and *halakah* that the Apostle Paul takes his monumental stand in the letter to the Galatians when he announces that the purpose of the law is to "lead us to Christ" (Gal. 3:22-27). This stand means that Christians are "free!" Yes, they are free to be responsible; free to walk by the Spirit; free to walk with God "in newness of life" (Gal. 5:1-14). Paul, perhaps more than any other writer in the New Testament, sees the weakness of rabbinic Judaism's moral thinking. He also catches Jesus' vision for developing a Christian ethic and its relationship to an authentic life.

to Jerusalem to be firmly educated by one of the most elite teachers of Judaism, Gamaliel (a revered scholar in the tradition of Hillel). But after an episodic meeting with the risen Jesus, this Saul/Paul became one of Christianity's most dynamic spokespersons. He refused to back down to anyone—including the earlier disciples such as James, Peter, and John (cf. Gal. 2:6-10)—concerning God's free gift of salvation in Jesus and apart from all forms of legalism. To make that message known, he traveled thousands of miles throughout the

Mediterranean world and suffered incredible hardships for Christ (cf. 2 Cor. 11:22-29). Moreover, he did it all because of his overwhelming gratitude to Jesus for giving him new life and an indomitable hope in the Resurrection (1 Cor. 9:15-23, 15:12-28).

Paul was ready to do battle with the forces of evil and the devil for the sake of Jesus and his free gift of salvation—but not for anything less than the gospel itself! Perhaps that kind of commitment is an important lesson we all need to learn so that we do not waste our energies and the resources of the church by engaging in fruitless battles that will not lead to the salvation of humans from the grip of Satan.

What are the foci of the recent battles in the church?

With these comments as a background, I turn to our recent "battles" in the church—battles focused on the Bible. I remember vividly an experience that alerted me to the great pain that such battles can create. It was at a dialogue meeting sponsored by the Lutheran World Federation and the Baptist World Alliance that took place at the Missouri Synod Lutheran Seminary (Concordia) in St. Louis. At that meeting about ten Lutherans and ten Baptists met to discuss their commonalities and differences.

Although the meeting was very cordial, there was a significant tension present. Interestingly, it was not between Lutherans and Baptists but between the Lutherans. It was the first time that two former professors from Concordia were sitting in the same room with their earlier colleagues after their denomination had split because of their "Battle for the Bible." It was very painful to watch. I said to my colleague, the late George R. Beasley-Murray of England: "I pray that this type of battle never comes to Baptists." But it did come! And it came with a vengeance for Baptists, the segment of Protestants that has produced a huge force of missionaries. Unfortunately for Christ's work, the impact has been very serious but not always acknowledged.

I could detail the many conflicts that have arisen and the justifications that have been offered by both sides in the wake of these battles, but I will not do so because such a further enhancement of these battles would only bring glory to Satan and his minions. Indeed, even an outline of the harm that has resulted to church congregations, institutions, and people is staggering. And the shallow public defenses that have followed have left many people, especially young adults, with grave doubts about the integrity of the church. While many of those who have engaged in such battles may be convinced that they have defended the integrity of the Bible in the name of God, I am fairly sure that there will be great surprises in store for many who will be confronted by a stern-faced God in the time of judgment. We should all remember the words of Peter that "judgment begins in the household of God" (1 Pet. 4:17).

How are Christians in general dealing with the battles in the church?

In moving to the conclusion of this letter, we need to ponder some further questions, for example:

- What has happened since the time of Jesus and the early church?
- Have we forgotten the message of the Beatitudes (Matt. 5:1-12)?
- Have we chosen, instead, to follow the devil and the ways of the world—especially in our admiration and adoption of fighting patterns in the church?
- Do we really believe that battles and wars can solve human problems?
- Do we think that such battles actually bring people closer to Jesus?
- Did our recent battles for the Bible make the Bible more trustworthy in the church and for the world, *or* did they just make lifelong enemies among Christians?
- Did the battles for the Bible build unity in the church *or* split churches?
- During the battles for the Bible, did the world see in the newspapers and on the television a loving church fervently proclaiming a loving Christ, *or* did the world witness self-centered Christians grasping for attention and people filled with anger and resentment?

Then, a further question needs to be posited: Should we as Christians be doing battle? I believe the answer is: definitely yes. But maybe we should be doing battle with evil and the devil and not vilifying other Christians.

Do you recall that interesting exchange Jesus had with the early disciple John in Mark 9:38-41 when John tells Jesus about another person—not in their group—who is casting out demons in the name of Jesus? In defense of Jesus, John forbids him from doing so! But Jesus responds to John that he is badly misguided in trying to protect Jesus from someone else doing work in the name of Jesus. Such a person is clearly not against Jesus. I fear that we in the church have a great deal to learn about who is on the Lord's side. I fear we often mistake who is our enemy. In our self-righteous battles we might be fighting against God and the divine will!

Now, in answering the questions about Christian warfare, I am in no way suggesting that we should treat the Bible haphazardly or as unimportant. The Bible is crucial for providing us with God-given insights into the way we should live authentically in this world. But we must be acutely aware that Jesus severely rebuked the religious leaders who used the words of the Bible and the name of God for their own purposes while actually caring little for genuine love, integrity, humility, and piety.

Remember, it was the religious people who sought to kill Jesus. I wonder if he came back to the church today whether or not we might try to do battle with him and attempt to kill him—again! So, I charge you: Make sure that if you engage in a battle against evil, know who is your partner and who is your real enemy.

May God give us all divine wisdom as we encounter disputes and divisions among Christians, and may the Lord enlighten us as we seek to engage in various ministries within our churches and in our faith communities. Let us be sure that we follow the Spirit of Jesus who pronounced a series of blessings on the dispossessed as identified in the Sermon on the Mount (Matt. 5:1-12). And let us be sure we are on the side of the Lord who commended those who were loving and caring but condemned to eternal punishment those who failed to treat people with genuine care in his final sermon on the Mount of Olives (Matt. 26:4-46). These teachings are not just idle words; they indicate that our destinies are at stake.

In Christ Jesus,
Dad / Dr. B.

Questions for Reflection

- Is it possible that both God and the devil could be at work in your church? Why or why not?
- Do you think the battles for the Bible were inspired by God or the devil? Why? What point was Dr. B. trying to make about people using chaos to achieve their goals?
- Read again Matthew 23:13-36 and respond to this question: Why do you think Jesus was so harsh on the religious leaders of his time?
- Why do you think Dr. B. did not want to detail what he knew about the battles for the Bible in his circles?

- Why do you think Dr. B. inserted the excursus on "Walking with God" into this section of "Battles"? What could be the implications for our interpreting the Bible today?
- As you reflect on your church/faith community/denomination, are there any battles or conflicts taking place? If there are, what can you do about such conflicts?

Notes

[1]Harold Lindsell sounded his war cry for the late twentieth century in America with his book, *The Battle for the Bible* (Grand Rapids: Zondervan, 1976).

[2]See Louis Finkelstein's excellent treatment, *The Pharisees: The Sociological Background of Their Faith*, 3rd ed., 2 vols. (Philadelphia: The Jewish Publication Society of America, 1962), 1:74-114. For a brief summary of the Jewish parties in the time of Jesus, see Gerald L. Borchert, *Jesus of Nazareth: Background, Witnesses, and Significance* (Macon, GA: Mercer University Press, 2011), 59-65.

Chapter 5

Political Realities and Government

Dear Mark, Tim, and Friends:

Having tangentially dealt with politics in the context of several other questions, I now will deal with this issue more directly.

How should Christians relate to government and politics in their context?

The issue of politics and government is not an easy matter to discuss because of the intense feelings that often flow from the mere mention of the subject. Many Christians would rather avoid the issue of politics completely because of its controversial nature and the potential for upsetting relationships. Yet it is important to address the subject of how Christians relate to the political dynamics and their views of government in their time and context.

I approach this issue with the firm belief that all citizens need to be involved in the political process and that Christians should be able to voice their views if they are free to do so and very carefully if they are in settings where they are not free to express their opinions openly without endangerment. I also approach the subject as a former lawyer who has been involved in various aspects of the political process and has known what other lawyers have thought of the fact that I had a very small picture of Jesus facing me on my desk just to remind me (not others) to be an authentic Christlike person in such relationships. I believe firmly that Christians are Christ's people and that they should take Christ into their daily activities, but should do so gently and charitably without making a great show of it. In reflecting on the issues in this section, I have pondered and sought to find a Christlike way to discuss these matters, although I am cognizant of the fact that almost everything we say and do has political ramifications and can alienate some people.

What do you think Dr. B. learned in his study and research of the Hitler era while in Germany?

I have had the opportunity to teach a number of New Testament seminars at a seminary that was once located in Hamburg, Germany and has now moved to the outskirts of Berlin. There I had the special opportunity to research the Hitler era. It is with this latter experience that I wish to begin my reflections.

A couple of decades after World War II ended, as the dean of an American seminary, I decided to take several extended visits to our sister seminary in Germany. While there, I attended a seminar on the rise and fall of Nazi Germany. It was for me a grand education into the relationships forged between the churches and the Hitler government.

The entwining relationships created at that time made it impossible for many church leaders to be the voice of Christian integrity to the nation. But I am grateful for those dissenting voices that were still there or who had escaped and sought to remind the church from outside concerning its true calling. Among those dissenters was my former professor, Otto A. Piper of Princeton, for whom I served as a teaching and research fellow. He had been given twenty-four hours to get out of Germany because of his writings on Christian ethics.

During my several times in Germany, I talked with the nursing sisters (Baptist nuns) who were alive during the Hitler era about their experiences. They were indeed gentle spirits, assuring me that they would wish no one harm. Yet they clearly had supported Hitler during his rise to power because he promised to clean up the state, get rid of the "gypsy problem," and close the brothels for which Hamburg as a port city was famous (and still is). For much of the Nazi period, the sisters seemed to have been unaware of how ruthless Hitler actually was, although they knew he had been rounding up the Jews—which they found abhorrent.

The principal/president at the seminary in Hamburg gave me free access to the seminary archives. As I was going through the files, I came across a picture that almost made my heart stop: one of a former principal with whom I had corresponded briefly after the war. From that picture it was as clear that the principal was wearing a Nazi brown shirt. That picture raised a number of stunning and frustrating questions that begged answers. I began to ask myself: What sacrifice would a Christian leader have to make to join such a demonic force? What would I have done if I were in that principal's shoes?

I had wondered about the man's dictatorial style from my correspondence with him and from the reports I had received from a couple of our former students who had been exchange students there under his tenure after the war. I had also wondered why it was so much easier for me to deal with his two successors. Then, as the questions and responses came together, the answer began to dawn on me: The Autobahn ran right next to the seminary, but took a slight curve just before it reached the seminary. Oh my, I thought, he saved the seminary from being bulldozed. But what was the cost of saving the bricks and mortar—and perhaps the students too?

Those questions have continued to weigh on my mind as I have tried to reflect on how many church leaders in America, like those in Germany, have played with politics and power in the name of God. Some of them have maintained a fairly balanced and authentic role as both church leaders representing the way of God and as citizens representing their own political views. But many others have been far less authentic and pandering to politicians in seeking favors from them and overlooking personal and political waywardness while proclaiming support for those leaders and their policies and practices. Although human governments are not the Kingdom of God, to represent that divine kingdom is the duty and calling of all Christians. For Christians to do anything less is to miss the mark as followers of Jesus.

During my time in Germany, I also visited and spoke at a number of churches where people seemed to be quite authentic. I noticed that many of their buildings were not very ornate, so I began to ask questions. I assumed that many of the churches had been bombed and were continuing in the refurbishing process, but I learned a surprising lesson in those encounters.

Coming from the United States where many churches display an American flag, I asked why there was no German flag in their worship centers or in the narthex of their buildings. Then the people unfolded their stories to me: They had been so convicted by their compromising in the Nazi period, they did not want a national flag in their worship centers! Their first and primary loyalty was to Jesus. They were Germans, but Christ was their "Fuehrer!" "Wow," I thought, "that practice should be a forceful warning to me and to American churches." As a Christian, I am firmly committed to the separation of church and state, but these people provided me with a radical demonstration of such an approach. Maybe there is a lesson here for us in North America.

As I have reflected on the populism in the Hitler era and some patterns in the politics of other countries where I have visited and taught, I firmly believe that populism is usually founded on the genuine desire to affirm the truth of fundamental values in the midst of chaos and the loss of core values, particularly in a decadent society. But it can easily become twisted to eliminate certain people who are regarded as the scapegoats. They easily become the punching bags of an insecure and lazy society that longs for the return of their particular core values. But in the hands of dictatorial leaders such as Hitler, the call for a return of values can be used as a hidden means for the elimination of core freedoms that are basic to a democracy.

I think it would be of great value for you to peruse and ponder Hitler's summons to the German people, *Mein Kampf*, with his twisting of reality in mind.[1] Many people said after the Second World War that such a pattern could never happen again, but people in democracies and in free societies are often lazy, forget history, and fail to understand the nature of chaos and how chaos can be used inappropriately. Takeover by dictators can happen in any free society, whether they are nations or political and religious organizations. It can even happen within churches. Free people must be responsible and be on guard for such patterns of choosing specific persons and groups to blame when chaos is present. This story about Germany leads me to the next question.

Are there any biblical guidelines for Christians in relating to political realities?

I believe the answer is a definite yes. When I reflect on the First Epistle of Peter, I have a feeling that this transformed follower of Jesus is signaling such a perspective. Just check his brilliant triad in chapter 2: "Honor" all people; "love" your Christian brothers and sisters; "fear" God (v. 17). Do you sense the pyramid of response? What about the emperor? Notice that the response in 1 Peter is: "Honor" the emperor!

The emperor deserved respect, but he was not God—nor was he to be equated with the Christian church. The implication of that statement applies to all political leaders, even today. Our political leaders should never be identi- fied—even closely—with the divine. Political leaders are not God. That is the reason I completely reject the historical notion of the divine right of kings. Political leaders who use their authority wisely serve the will of God, as Paul correctly observes in Romans 13. But when they misuse their power, they are under the spell of the evil one, as John in Revelation 13 observes.

What then shall I say about Christians and American politics? I think the slogan "God and Country" has some value as a handy summary of some of our core values, but this slogan must be carefully nuanced because God and country should never be viewed on the same level by Christians. Furthermore,

I fear that in this "me-centered" generation many people (even Christians) have demoted both "God" and "country" in order to use both God and country for their own benefits. We are a narcissistic people, and for many in America the "I" or the "me" is their God. When the self becomes "god," all hell can break loose. That is what we found with Hitler in Germany. Could it happen again elsewhere?

I do not label myself—even though some may label me—as one of those "evangelicals" who became popular in the previous era or generation. Many of these have sold their souls for a little attention from politicians and for a few legal tidbits. That is what happened in Nazi Germany to the Lutherans, Baptists, and other Christians who were not part of the "Confessing Church." Having compromised with Hitler, those Christians lost their ability to proclaim the need for justice and righteousness. This can happen again among Christians in our growing secular world. Many have become fearful of taking stands on justice issues and are silent in the face of the abuse of power because they might lose their standing with political leaders. They fail to confront those who prey on the marginalized, just as Christians were silent during the Nazi pogrom when Hitler tried to eliminate the Jews and gypsies.

Like our compatriots throughout the centuries, we Christians of today often fail to challenge the power politics of the status quo. But the question before us is this: Are we "fair weather" Christians? Or, are we willing to take seriously the Old Testament model testimonies where the prophets dared to stand against the governing authorities. Consider Nathan's confrontation of David for his immorality (2 Sam. 12:1-14) and Jeremiah's multiple dictations to Baruch concerning the fierce condemnations of the Lord for Jehoiakim (Jer. 36:1-32). Of course, such actions were daring, but there was a serious possibility of reprisal. Jeremiah's life hardly had a happy, fairy-tale ending.

While little is recorded by the evangelists concerning Jesus confronting the political powers of his day, the brief snippets concerning his encounters with Herod and Pilate give us clues to how he would have reacted. One point is especially significant: When Pilate thought he was in charge, Jesus—as a prisoner—boldly announced to the Roman procurator that he would have no power except that it had been given "from above" (John 19:11). The lives of politicians revolve around the issue of power. Pilate was clearly in the power quest to become "a friend of Caesar" (19:12). The Jews knew it and used it for their own benefit. Jesus knew it and confronted Pilate on that very issue of power.

In other examples, John the Baptist revealed his God-oriented commitment when he confronted Herod Antipas for his lousy lifestyle. John paid for challenging the king's personal affairs with his imprisonment and ultimately his death (Matt. 14:3-11, Luke 3:19-20). Similarly, Paul, even as a prisoner, did not hesitate to confront Felix, the Roman procurator, and his wife Drusilla, directly concerning their despicable personal lives (Acts 24:25).

Can we evaluate the church and Christians in relation to political realities today?

In light of these texts, I have been asking some thorny questions about myself and other Christians today in relation to politics: Why would we, as Christians, prefer to pander and praise politicians rather than hold them to high standards of morality and integrity? Do our actions (or inactions) say something about who we really are? Maybe it is time for some Christian personal soul-searching.

Perhaps there is another question related to Christians and politics. Could we as Christians be not too unlike some of the rabbis in Jesus' day who mouthed God's transforming message of acceptance for the rejects of society while they stood aloof from those who were actually crying to them for hope and help? I pray that such is not the case with us in the church today, but if we act like those rabbis, we also deserve the scathing attack Jesus delivered to the Pharisees in Matthew 23: Woe to you hypocrites . . . Woe to you blind guides . . . Woe to you whitewashed tombs . . . You snakes . . .

I do not like those condemnations. We cannot and must not abandon our divine calling to be a caring and redeeming community within our society, and we dare not exchange that calling of Christ for a bowl of compromising pottage—similar to that red stuff Esau ate in exchange for his birthright (Gen. 25:34)! If we do not heed the cries that are coming from the world, we may soon find our churches grasping for meaning and purpose. We have been given a twofold summons to preach the good news of forgiveness and to care for the rejects of society. Our call is similar to that of Jesus who both proclaimed salvation in the Kingdom of God and fed hungry stomachs, and it is parallel to the fact that he healed the sick and forgave sins. The gospel is holistic, and to such a gospel we are all called—even in the way we think and act in the realm of politics.

While I may be a little concerned for the current health of the church today, I firmly anticipate that God will again renew the church and will raise up voices who will speak an authentic word not only to those who are within the church but also to our governments and to our politicians.

One of those agents could be you. The world is suffering from multiple chaotic factors, and our governments are reflecting that chaos. Let us pray for more order and harmony to come to our country and for a divine answer to the hostile attitudes and disunity that are tearing at the hearts of our people.

In Christ,
Dad / Dr. B.

Questions for Reflection

- What were your reactions to Dr. B.'s details about the Baptist nuns and the principal of the German seminary during the Hitler era?
- What do you think about Dr. B.'s discussion of German and American flags? Where do you stand on such an issue?
- How do you react to holding politicians (local and national) *and* ministers and church leaders responsible for high standards of integrity?
- Why is chaos a useful tool used by dictators to accomplish their goals? How does chaos play into the diminishing of freedom? How should Christians react to the diminishing of freedom?
- Do you have different standards for the political party you favor over against the political party you oppose?
- How do you relate to the poor, the weak, and the dispossessed in society? Do you think American churches and Christians care about the poor and the dispossessed? Do you think that caring for the dispossessed is the task of our government? Of churches? Do you think those tasks are interrelated? How?

Note

[1]See various reprints of Hitler's *Mein Kampf* in English as *My Struggle: Four and Half Years of Struggle Against Lies, Stupidity, and Cowardice*, translated by James Murphy in 1939 and republished in 2007 and released by Create Space Independent Publishing Platform, various dates such as 2014.

Chapter 6

The Meaning of Salvation

Dear Mark, Tim, and Friends:

We now come to some of the key questions concerning how we seek to understand what it means to be a Christian.

How should we understand salvation?

Questions on salvation are basic to what we believe and how we act as Christians. I have repeatedly been asked questions concerning salvation—about being saved, when it happens, and if one can be saved and then not saved. This present response is not about theological differences advocated by various denominations, nor is it about the theological creeds and confessions of denominations—although it could have an impact on how we view our statements and creeds. In this discussion I want to focus on some intriguing ideas I have discovered in the writings of the Apostle Paul and how his views can influence the way we think about salvation. So, let me begin with a cute little apocryphal story I heard while studying at Princeton many years ago.

Two Scottish theologians were walking down a street in Edinburgh when they were confronted by a Salvation Army officer who was seeking to converse with them. The officer asked, "Brothers, are you saved?" The one theologian thought briefly and then replied, "Yes, partly, and no!" Bewildered, the SA officer gasped, "What?" The theologian's response came back, "Yes, I am justified. Partly, I am sanctified. And no, I am not glorified!"

While this story is catchy, it makes some precise points that can assist us in clarifying thinking among Christians who have a slightly truncated view of salvation. The Christian view of salvation involves far more than walking down the aisle of a church and saying "Yes" to an evangelistic invitation. That is only the introduction to the first stage in one's life of faith or the road to salvation. And that course of salvation is not an easy, quick race to the finish.

It is a long marathon of living with God under the guidance of the Holy Spirit, as the preacher of the Book of Hebrews proclaims (cf. Heb. 12:1-29).

The three words that the Scottish theologian used with the SA officer are significant and actually represent three aspects of salvation in the letters of Paul. Indeed, these terms represent not merely aspects of salvation, but actually three stages of salvation. Moreover, these stages are an example of the way Paul thinks in triads.

How does Paul's use of triads help us in explaining the Christian life and salvation?

Paul often thinks in sets of three concerning humans in their lives and actions. His letter to Thessalonians contains a number of such triads. The most familiar one is in 1 Corinthians 13: faith, hope, and love (v. 13). But these three are not in the best chronological order when we reflect about salvation.

"Faith" is often linked with justification or the initial stage of salvation, though faith is necessary throughout life. "Love" is partnered with sanctification or the second stage, which involves living out the implications of the life of faith. And "hope" is paired with glorification, or the third and future stage of the Christian's life.

The order of the words in the triad vary, depending on Paul's intentions in a particular letter. But when Paul uses this familiar triad in a letter, the final term in this three-word series seems to provide an important clue as to what stage of the salvation process may be Paul's primary concern or focus in that letter.

Naturally, since Paul was usually writing to Christians and, if he used the triad, we would assume that faith (the initial stage of salvation) would generally appear first and not at the end of any sequence. And I have not as yet found such a sequence that ends with faith. The place where we might expect to find it third in such an order would be in the bombastic letter to the Galatians. But the threefold summary of salvation is not there. And as I have argued in my commentary, I am convinced that Galatians was the first letter (extant) we have from Paul.[1] It is the place where he clarified his early thinking, and I am quite sure that his thoughts in this letter parallel what must have been his basic argument in the Jerusalem Council. It must have served as the foundation for the strategic decision that the Gentiles did not need to become Jews—or be circumcised—in order to become Christians (Acts 15).

What is the point of the Book of Galatians?

In the explosive opening to Galatians, Paul is ready to hurl a dooming curse (*anathema*) against anyone, even an angel from heaven, who might attempt to preach about salvation other than by faith in Jesus Christ—an idea he once tried to obliterate (Gal. 1:6-9, 12, 23). Indeed, the passion of the persecutor probably birthed for early Christianity its foremost apologist or preacher of the gospel—the one who challenged the thought patterns and faithfulness of even the earlier followers of Jesus such as James, Peter, and John (Gal. 2:9). Indeed, elsewhere Paul claims that he worked harder than all of them (1 Cor. 15:11).

With the passion of a fighting crusader, Paul then charges the "stupid Galatians" with succumbing to a bewitching spell of evil and abandoning the faith that brought them to Jesus Christ and life in the Spirit (Gal. 3:1-5). Instead, he insists that they are turning back to the fruitless way of rules and regulations to gain God's approval—when they already have it in Christ! Indeed, they could be counted as heirs of Abraham through Jesus Christ to whom the law has been pointing (3:6-29). Then, seemingly summoning every ounce of energy within him, he proclaims: "For freedom, Christ has set you free . . . so, don't submit again to the yoke of slavery" (5:1). Instead, he insists, "walk by the Spirit . . . and abandon the way of your sinful nature" (6:16). What a magnificent manifesto on faith! But it is not Paul's most complete statement on the subject. That statement comes in his later letter to the Romans in which he expands on his understanding of salvation.

How does the Book of Romans expand our understanding of salvation in terms of the way we live and act?

In Paul's more sophisticated work of Romans—the trumpet call of the Reformation—the salvation triad appears, but not in chapters 1–4 where Paul writes a great deal about faith. That discussion on faith, however, is preliminary to his primary concern about living the Christian life. Accordingly, in Romans 5 he presupposes that his recipients have been justified by "faith" (v. 1). Then, as in the 1 Corinthians 13 triad, Paul mentions "hope" (v. 2) and concludes with "love" (v. 5). Chapters 6–8 focus on living out the implications of baptism, moving forward in our struggles as Christians, and yielding our lives to the leading of the Spirit—all of which are directed to understanding the sanctified life (cf. 6:19), the end of which, Paul states, will ultimately lead to eternal life (6:22).

The point for Paul is that the justified person is duty-bound not to let sin have control of the Christian's life (6:12). But Paul is also fully aware that transformation will not be complete in this life and that there is a war going on in Christians (7:22). Clearly, he knows that justified people will continue to wrestle with the realities of sin and will not always do what is good—not even when they desire to do so (7:13-20). Moreover, they might at times feel traumatized by not measuring up to their desires to do the divine will and in exasperation call on God for deliverance from their continued failures (7:24-25). Nevertheless, they can be assured that God is not looking at them like a stern judge but as a compassionate savior who will not condemn them (8:1). The Lord will instead continue to stand beside them in their struggles and lead them to walk under the guidance of the Spirit of God (8:3-5, 10-11). The constant presence of the Spirit, thus, is their trustworthy resource that enables them to deal with failure, even exasperation (8:18-27), and they can be assured that while they live in this mortal life nothing in all creation can separate them from the love of God that is in Christ Jesus (8:39).

How do chapters 9–11 of the Book of Romans fit into Paul's discussion?

Romans 9–11 is one of the most misunderstood and avoided sections in all of Paul's writing. This Scripture is a unique part of his thinking about salvation—namely, his own unanswered questions. Paul knows that the people of Israel (the Jews) are Abraham's natural heirs and that Abraham was God's model of faith (4:3), so he is concerned with why they did not accept Jesus, God's chosen agent of salvation. While Paul does not reach a satisfactory conclusion, he does arrive at a partial answer—namely, that not all the descendants of Abraham and Jacob (Israel) are genuinely spiritual heirs of Abraham (9:6).

But that answer does not satisfy Paul, so he begins to argue with himself as he latches on to the subject of election and the fact that God is like a potter who seeks to mold his people to the divine will (9:11, 19-33). Yet, while this proposition reflects God's promises and action, it is not the whole answer because, for Paul, it does not take into account the human will. Accordingly, he returns to the necessity of faith and believing in chapter 10 and asserts the need for people both to "confess that Jesus is Lord" and to "believe . . . that God raised him from the dead." And then, so as to emphasize the importance of these two actions for followers of Christ, Paul repeats himself by reversing these two actions as the basis for salvation (10:9-10). To punctuate the importance of this statement, he makes sure his readers understand that there are not two ways to salvation. He does so by adding his repeated refrain that there is no distinction between Jew and Greek. All people must follow through in calling on the Lord in order to be saved (10:12-13).

But what about Paul's worrisome question related to the Jews? Have they been rejected? His answer is a resounding "No." Paul himself is a Jew, a descendant of Abraham (11:1). The opposite conclusion would imply that God had canceled his promise to Abraham. So, Paul reminds his readers that God always has a remnant who remain faithful (11:4; see his reference to the 7,000 who did not bow to a false god in 1 Kgs. 19:18). The answer Paul deduces has to be in a temporary hardening of Israel against Jesus so that the Gentiles can be accepted (Rom. 11:7-12).

While this answer does not totally satisfy Paul, he recognizes that God wanted to bless all the nations through Abraham (cf. Gen. 12:1-3). That is the reason Paul adopts the two metaphors of the dough and the grafting of olive branches. The image of dough implies that when truly Christlike Gentiles are mixed with truly Christlike people of Israel or Jews, then the dough eliminates distinctions of acceptability or holiness. The image of the grafting and removal of olive branches is a little more developed and, even though it may not represent the best current horticultural practices,[2] it provides a helpful commentary on how Paul envisages an answer to his troubling question— namely, by the insertion of the Gentiles (unnatural branches) into the root of Abraham and the temporary removal of Israel (the natural branches) from the root (Rom. 11:17-24). Then he envisions that the Jews would become envious of the Gentile acceptance by God and would want to accept God's provision of Jesus as the answer (11:14).

Having thus settled on this picture as the best solution to his nagging question, Paul then employs the image of God as pruner to remind his Gentile readers that they should pay attention and understand both "the kindness and severity of God" (11:22). They should take great care and not become haughty because they too could be cut out of Abraham's stalk.

This text, therefore, is a serious warning for Christians to be faithful in living authentically and following the leading of the Holy Spirit. It is also a serious challenge to the popular theological slogan of "once saved always saved," which is not found in the Bible and is simply a myth constructed from the more nuanced concept of the perseverance of the saints.

Still, Paul is convinced that the Jews will not ultimately reject Christ and he posits that they will ultimately accept Jesus as their answer to life and be restored. He concludes this section concerning his nagging question about the Jews with an inspiring doxology concerning the mysterious and awesome nature of God whose actions in saving humans are beyond human understanding (11:33-36).

Paul closes his letter with a series of instructions intended to foster holy living and integrity before God. Like most of 1 Corinthians (which I briefly introduced with a reference to the salvation triad), both come from the middle period of Paul's ministry and focus on the middle stage of salvation that emphasizes living the Christian life.

How do 1 Thessalonians and Colossians enlighten us about preparing for the final stage of salvation?

When we turn to 1 Thessalonians (probably written after Galatians), the order of the triad differs from 1 Corinthians and Romans. The focus is also different. Notice in 1:3 that the order is "faith," "love," and "hope"—which alerts us to the concern with eschatology or the last stage of salvation. Moreover, in the same paragraph Paul further illuminates this triad by formulating another parallel triad in 1:9-10. There he states that these Macedonian believers have turned to God (the initial stage that involves a major change in life), intend to serve the living God (the second stage of moving forward in the life of obedience and sanctification), and await the coming of God's Son (the final stage which is to be with the Lord; cf. 4:17).

The focus in 1 Thessalonians seems to be quite clear. Paul's concern for these Christians is to help them deal with their disturbing questions of death prior to the *parousia* (presence or return) of Jesus. He does not want them to worry about their future with God. Painfully, they are seeing their colleagues dying like non-Christians and are asking questions about why Christ has not yet come. Therefore, Paul wants to assure them that the future of those who have died in Christ is absolutely secure because the dead will be raised and not miss the trumpet call of God (4:13-18).

Paul is clearly aware that death seems to be so final to humans, but for him the Resurrection of Jesus is God's visible assurance that the Christian hope is not a mere mythical fairy tale (1:10; cf. the long discourse on the resurrection in 1 Corinthians 15). Accordingly, this letter to the Thessalonians is a powerful message of consolation to the distressed. And just as it provided a magnificent message of comfort (1 Thess. 4:18) and encouragement (5:11) to the early Greek believers, it continues to do so for countless Christians through the ages.

I turn now to consider how a letter from the closing period in Paul's life can enlighten us concerning the final stage of salvation. I regard Colossians as the pinnacle of Paul's Christology.[3] Paul undoubtedly wrote this missive while in prison, and in such a setting he was likely contemplating the probability of his forthcoming death. In this letter he again uses the triad with the order of "faith," "love," and "hope" in the opening chapter at verses 4 and 5. We may therefore anticipate that his focus will be on the last stage of salvation.

Almost immediately after referring to the triad, Paul seems to pass into a reflective mood in which he meditates on the extension of the gospel throughout the world and how it has been fruitful and transformed lives even in a place such as Colossae where he has never visited (1:6-7). For this growth he is exceedingly grateful, and he prays that Christians in that area will be empowered and will understand the amazing benefits of the gospel that provide them with both their deliverance from evil and their inheritance in the kingdom of God (1:9-14). These thoughts must have consciously led Paul to expound on the incredible nature of Christ in one of the most elevated Christological statements in the New Testament (Col. 1:15-20; cf. also Heb. 1:1-3, John 1:1-18, Rev. 1:1-20).

But notice that although Paul's mind is wrapped in the transcendent vision of the preeminent Christ who has been active in the creation of everything and who should be regarded as the reconciling answer to all concerns, still Paul's feet are firmly planted in the troubled world. With the perspective of this divine vision in mind, Paul turns in the rest of the letter to his eschatological goal and calls on believers to eschew all forms of evil and divisiveness since Christ has triumphed over the principalities and powers in the world (2:15). Then Paul summons believers to fulfill their baptismal commitments and put on the various attributes of Christ, including love (3:12-14), so that the long-awaited "peace of Christ" might rule in their hearts (3:15). As a result, they will demonstrate the goal of the Lord's Prayer that the will of God "be done on earth as it is in heaven" (cf. Matt. 6:10)—because they will do everything "in the name of the Lord Jesus" (Col. 3:17).

What are the implications of such a full three-stage view of salvation for our lives as Christians?

As a result of this detailed discussion of several Pauline letters, I trust you understand more clearly why that cute little apocryphal story about the two Scottish theologians actually supplies some crucial insights into the breadth of salvation that is often missed by our simple questions about being saved. Yes, we can be declared acceptable to God through Christ's self-giving death and resurrection for us. That is a wonderful message!

But that is not the full story of salvation, as Paul struggled to make clear to the early believers. There is much more to the story. So, I would strongly challenge you to remind others in our contemporary world that salvation with the coming of Jesus was never meant to be a "quick fix" treatment through some simple prescription of "religious pills" that might deliver us from life's problems.

Salvation is instead a lifelong journey of walking with God in Christ through the Spirit. Yes, it does start with faith—believing in the personal coming to earth of the self-giving Jesus, God's only Son, who freely took upon himself the sins of humanity in the crucifixion and who was raised again to confirm the divine authorization of our salvation. This same Jesus will surely come again as we wait in expectation for that glorious eschatological meeting with our risen Savior. In the meantime, however, we who have faith in the risen Lord are advised to walk carefully in love and newness of life and work with integrity for Christ. We are strictly warned against setting our minds on the way of the flesh (focusing on things of this world), and we are clearly advised not to turn away from the leading of God (Rom. 8:4-14, Gal. 5:16-22), as the Jews and all humanity repeatedly have been doing.

Nevertheless, in spite of our unfaithfulness, we can be assured that Christ continues to remain faithful and is ever present in our lives to welcome and reaffirm us in our relationship with the Lord when we stumble—unless we banish him from our presence. But it is up to us to be responsible to God in all our thoughts and actions and to live authentically in the world by demonstrating in our own lives Christ's model of this self-giving love to others whom we encounter.

God bless you as you follow the leading of the Lord in your lives and as you seek to touch others with the gracious love of Christ.

In Christian love,
Dad / Dr. B.

Questions for Reflection

- Do you find the way Dr. B. deals with the triad of faith, love, and hope to be helpful and enlightening? Why or why not?
- How do you react to the way Dr. B. presents the difficult text of Romans 9–11? What points do you think Paul was trying to make in those chapters?
- After reflecting on each of the terms "faith," "love," and "hope," how would you summarize the significance of each one? What impact does this combination make in the way you view Paul's understanding of salvation?
- Why do you think Dr. B. is warning his readers against viewing salvation as a "quick fix," "once for all time" answer to the problem of human sin?
- What view(s) concerning salvation do you think are truncated and do not represent authentic Christian understandings?

Notes

[1]Gerald L. Borchert, "Galatians" in Roger Morlang and Gerald L. Borchert, *Romans and Galatians*, vol. 14, Cornerstone Biblical Commentary (Carol Stream, IL: Tyndale House, 2007), 248-251.

[2]While I would not suggest that I know much about being an oleiculturalist, yet from what I have learned, grafting is a very difficult process for inserting olive branches into old plants. Nevertheless, the illustration provides a vivid example Paul was using to describe the relationship between Gentiles and Jews.

[3]For my further comments on Colossians, see Gerald L. Borchert, "Baptism and the Pinnacle of Pauline Christology: Paul's Letter to the Colossians," in *Portraits of Jesus for an Age of Biblical Illiteracy* (Macon, GA: Smyth and Helwys, 2016), 95-103.

Chapter 7

Defining a Christian

Dear Mark, Tim, and Friends:

Here is a question you may not have pondered:

Where in the Bible can we find the best definition of a Christian?

The best definition of a Christian is not found in the Gospel of John, nor in the other Johannine writings, the other Gospels, the Petrine letters, or the Book of James. And it is not in the Pauline works, although there is a detailed statement of the will of God for Christians in Romans. It is actually found in the context of one of the harshest warnings in the Bible: chapter 6 of the sermon called Hebrews.[1]

What is encompassed in the definition of a Christian given in Hebrews?

The Preacher of Hebrews[2] masterfully sets the stage for both his powerful warnings to humans and his defining of a Christian by introducing Jesus as the Son of God who bore the very image and nature of God (Heb. 1:1-3) and was far superior to all of God's angels (1:5-13). But this Jesus genuinely took on humanity and "tasted" or succumbed to death for everyone (2:19), and in his sacrificial death he demonstrated as a human (in his human nature) that he had the liberating authority to break the power of the devil and set humans free from their bondage to sin and assist them when they are tested/tempted (2:14-18). This powerful demonstration was a manifestation that he deserved more glory than all the mortals who may have crossed the Preacher's mind—including Moses (3:1-6), Joshua (4:8-10), and the high priest Aaron (4:14–5:5), except for the illusive Christlike figure of Melchizedek (5:6).

Then, like a bolt out of the blue and with a stunning turn, the Preacher announces that he could add more to his expositions on God's Son, but his readers (perhaps also his listeners) are too spiritually dull (like sleepyheads) and are still like babies who need milk rather than solid food (5:11-14). So instead of continuing the discussion on God's Son, he decides to deal with their nature as Christian believers and their need for maturity. So he begins by focusing on the need for going beyond the fundamental characteristics or presupposed doctrines related to Christ and the salvation of Christians (6:1-2), including:

• the need for repentance from dead works
• faith in God ("saving faith")
• instruction related to washings such as baptism
• the laying on of hands
• belief in the resurrection of the dead
• belief in eternal judgment

This list of six elements, taken as a unified whole, probably provides us later readers with a helpful summary about what the early church taught its new converts should be the basic doctrinal commitments of the community. Although this list is not detailed, any knowledgeable Christian should be able to complete it.

But the Preacher does not stop with this list of commitments to theological ideas: he wants his sleepyhead Christians to understand who they are and what their life commitments involve since his primary focus throughout the sermon is on obedience to Christ as their Lord.

So, in the second section of his reflection (6:4-6), he alters his focus slightly. The highlights of the second list in his message fall upon the characteristics of persons who evidence a living relationship with the Son of God. They are described as:

• Those who have been enlightened: They have turned from the dark ways of the world to the revealed Son of God.
• Those who have "tasted" the heavenly gift: They have imbibed or experienced the gracious gift of grace through God's Son and his transforming power in their lives. ("Taste" here does not mean that the gift simply touched the tip of their tongues, as some have argued, because that would mean that Jesus who tasted death (2:9) would not really have died.)
• Those who have become partakers or shared in the leading of the Holy Spirit
• Those who have tasted or received the goodness of God's word dwelling in them: They sense God's meaning and purposes of God's Son in their lives.
• Those who have tasted or experienced the powers of the age to come: They do not simply think in eschatological terms but are oriented to the future (after the end of time) and live in anticipation of Christ's return.

The impact of these two lists is almost overwhelming in their theological force and meaning. One might expect, therefore, that this Hebrews text would be quoted by all evangelists to those persons who are searching for what it means to be a Christian. But rather surprisingly these verses are generally avoided by those engaged in an evangelistic ministry of introducing people to Christ.

Why do ministers and evangelists rarely use these summaries of what it means to be a Christian?

These crucial summaries are avoided because the statement concerning the impossibility of being renewed again to repentance for "those who have once been enlightened" (6:4) is based on the condition "*if* they turn away (commit apostasy)," which means "they again crucify the Son of God and shame him publicly" (6:6). Yet, this statement is crucial to the Preacher's argument because living out our commitments even in the face of turmoil, threats, and persecution is a key to the Preacher's forceful message. Although he is fairly certain that his readers will not turn back on Jesus (6:9), he wants them to understand that Christian commitment is not a game that one can play with God and the world. The Preacher is serious in his message to these early Christians because of what is happening in their setting: Christians are being persecuted, exposed to public ridicule, and thrown into prison. Their property is being confiscated, and they are threatened with the possibility of death (10:13-16, 12:4).

Those of us who live today in the relative peace and security of North America may hardly begin to understand the harsh toll that was inflicted on those who endured long-term persecution, as the Christians in the Book of Hebrews were experiencing. Spiritual fatigue is a harsh life to face. The Preacher is aware of the plight of these Christians, and he takes great care to remind them of their earlier commitments to Christ. He knows that Christ died for them, but he also knows that God's Son died only once—not repeatedly to remove the curse of sin. Once for all people is the decisive message—the point of no return (6:6)! It is not an easy message.

This warning in Hebrews 6 is not the only warning in the Preacher's sermon. There are multiple warnings throughout the thirteen chapters, for example: "Pay attention . . . do not drift away" (2:1-2); "remain confident . . . don't harden your hearts" (3:6-7); "Take care . . . lest you fall away" (3:12); tremble with fear . . . lest some of you might fail" (4:1)—to name only a few. But his overarching point for these early believers is to take seriously that they have started their lives as "Christians." Completing the journey will take courage and perseverance (12:1-2). So, the Preacher reminds his readers that their Savior, Jesus, came once "to take away sins" and when he returns "he will not come again to deal with sins" but "to bring salvation." Yet between the present and the future prospect of their salvation there awaits the prospect of "judgment" (9:27-28).

Will these believers be ready for Christ's return, or will they fall away and abandon their faith and commitments to the Son of God? The Preacher knows the Christian life is hard for them. "Drifting away," "falling away," "rebelling," "hardening hearts," "becoming sluggish," "shrinking back," and "losing confidence" are all possibilities for followers of Jesus. The Preacher does not want them to fail to make it to the end when God will shake up everything so that only what is secure will survive and remain firm (12:26-29).

Can you give us more clarification on warnings in Hebrews?

Let me share the following excepts from both a recent letter with a question and my response to illustrate how Christians try to wrestle with the serious warnings in biblical texts and what those texts imply about being a Christian.

Dear Dr. B:

I have a PhD in computer science; I love God's Word; and I want to know and teach the truth. I am actively involved in missions, evangelism, and teaching . . . so the question I am asking you is not an idle question. . . . I was reading in your NAC commentary . . . about John 15:2. Your interpretation of "cuts away" or "takes away" was that those unproductive branches were "eliminated/taken away/removed." I imagine that you are probably aware of _____'s book . . . . In that book, he tells the story of a vineyard owner who "takes away" . . . those unproductive vines that are running along the ground, and muddy, are cleaned and moved to a higher location on the trellis/vine, and thus become fruitful.

								J

Dear J:

There are always those . . . who do not want to take the warning texts in Scripture seriously. Such a mindset does not want to admit that God could actually mean that once a person has confessed Jesus that the original confession must be less than authentic, if they turn away or are unproductive for the Lord. Those people will . . . insist that once one has made a serious confession, such a person is in the kingdom and will always be in the kingdom. The fallacy of such thinking is that it fails to take seriously the reality of the free will God has given to people. That theology also implies that God not only draws people to himself but also determines their decision to become a Christian. In my earlier book on assurance and warning I tried to make it clear that we need to take both ideas very seriously.[3] And we should not . . . try to explain away illustrations or statements that do not conform to the assurance texts. We make decisions for Christ, and we can also "tell God to go to H!" But if we do so, it is not God that is going there!

Perhaps you have never met a person who was on fire for Christ and then something happens to that person and he/she turns against God. . . . the warning texts of the Bible must be taken just as seriously as the assurance texts. Refusal to do so is one reason why so many . . . have difficulties with Hebrews and go through all sorts of explanations trying to justify that Hebrews does not really mean all the warnings that are in those texts. I believe in the security of those who want to remain faithful with God and that God will make ways for us to endure and deal with temptations (1 Cor. 10:13), but that does not mean that God will walk over a person's will. That is the reason I take the John 15 text seriously. God also can gather unfruitful branches and burn them. Remember, they are branches of the vine . . . . The human will is a mystery, but God does not deny our wills. If God superimposed his will on our will, we would all be automatons. And automatons cannot truly love! . . . .

I think this is enough of an explanation. God sent a wonderful model in Jesus for us to follow. We are hardly perfect, but someday by God's grace we will reach another reality which is beyond our comprehension now. Please do not play loose with the warnings in the Bible like some do. They are serious and are there for a reason . . .

This correspondence ended with a note from the inquiring party:

> Dear Dr. B. Thank you. . . . Your response is deep; I will have to read
> it many times. Thank you again. J

What guidance does the Book of Hebrews and other biblical texts offer Christians living under pressure?

As I have emphasized repeatedly to my students when we have studied this sermon of the Preacher, there is not just one "impossible" in the context of chapter 6, but two. The first is the impossibility of a second repentance following the public shaming of Christ (Heb. 6:6). The second is for God to prove false or lie. In this second impossible, God gives both a promise and an oath to the believers that will function as their anchor in the midst of life's struggles (6:19). That anchor is a divine symbol of hope for us weak mortals. In a similar vein, Paul also asserts that God is present in our trials and will provide a way for us to escape tragedy and avoid spiritual disaster *if* we rely on the Lord (cf. 1 Cor. 10:14).

I love this image of the "anchor." It contains the cross, and yet it speaks of security. When I took my dad to Israel to visit the places where Jesus lived and taught, we purchased an anchor for him to wear as a reminder that the Lord walked with him and promised never to leave him—even if he had to face truly difficult situations in the future.

Now, I am fully aware that many Christians do not like the warnings in this sermon called Hebrews because they fear that they might be in the hands of an angry God. But while God is not playing games, we should remember that it was God who in love sent Jesus to humans as the means of salvation, and that the fear of God is not necessarily negative if one trusts in Jesus. Such fear also provides security.

In the Book of Hebrews, the Preacher realizes that many of his Christian Jewish readers probably will not like his warnings—after all, they are children of the promises to Abraham. So, he takes special care to assure them that he knows the Old Testament message and its promises. But he also knows the weaknesses of their faith traditions. Their high priests were not perfect, but Christ was (Heb 7:26). Christ was like the intriguing Melchizedek to whom Abraham actually paid tithes (7:1-10). The accoutrements of their worship had never been perfect, but Christ's tent was not made by human hands (9:1-14). The sacrificial system that used the blood of animals required repetition and was hardly sufficient to take away sins, but Christ's sacrificial blood was shed only once for everyone (10:1-10). And at the center of the Preacher's argument stands the covenant itself with its laws that were not God's final intention for humans—even as Jeremiah 31:31-34 had predicted.[4] A new covenant was coming, and the laws would be written not on scrolls or on tablets of stone but on the hearts and minds of God's people. This new covenant has now been initiated through Christ, rendering the first covenant "obsolete" (Heb. 8:6-13). This new covenant in Christ is far superior to the earlier one.

Accordingly, I have great confidence in God that each one of us as Christians can avoid falling into inescapable tragedy from temptations or persecution when chaos and serious difficulties assail us—*if* we place our reliance on Christ and God's new covenant, not in ourselves. I also think it is intriguing and probably divinely inspired that the best definition for being a Christian in our sacred Scripture comes in a warning context concerning a Christian's potential for turning away from Jesus and denying him. Nevertheless, in this same context is God's promise to be our secure anchor that holds us in times of great distress and danger.

The Preacher of Hebrews is not alone in his concern for Christian integrity and stability. But as Matthew reminds us vividly in the defining Olivet discourse/sermon, Jesus is a judging shepherd who divides people into categories of sheep and goats at the last judgment. According to that text, persons who are convinced they will make it into the kingdom of heaven because of their works will be rejected by the Shepherd King. And on what basis will they be rejected? Their verbal confessions or theology? No! It will be on the basis of the way they lived and served others (Matt 26:41-46).

These warning texts may make us cringe if we have regarded our words as the sufficient test of our faithfulness. While our confessions are important, words without lives to support them will never be sufficient when it comes to the ultimate reckoning of humans by God. Reckoning a person to be a Christian and a follower of Jesus involves more than one's initial acceptance of Christ Jesus. The crucial word in this context is *endurance!* Do you think that the Preacher of Hebrews is alone in this perspective? That message goes back to Jesus himself (Mark 4:17, 13:13; Matt. 10:22; Luke 21:19) and to the rest of the New Testament where endurance is regarded as a crucial mark of Christian identity (Heb. 10:36; cf. Rom. 5:4, 2 Cor. 6:4, Jas. 1:12, Rev. 14:12, etc.).

Jesus realized that his followers would not normally have an easy life, so he made it clear that those who endure hostility and persecution to the end will be saved (Mark 13:11-13, Matt. 24:9-13). Early in his ministry the Apostle Paul called on the believers in Thessalonica to trust in God for the power to endure harassment and persecution (2 Thess. 1:4). And Paul personally learned through his own trials and sufferings—more than any of us would even dream of encountering—that to follow Jesus is very costly (2 Cor. 11:21-33). It was just as the Lord had foretold Ananias back in Damascus that Paul would suffer much (Acts 9:16). The harassments and persecution he endured were so intense that Paul admitted he almost gave up (2 Cor. 1:8). He felt like the sentence of death was upon him. But the resurrection of Jesus became for him his living symbol of the power that enabled him to believe in God's ability to deliver him (1:9-10).

The models of the anchor and of God's power revealed in the resurrection of Jesus should enable all Christians to be sustained in times of serious pain and suffering so that their identity as Christians will never be compromised. Indeed, Paul tells us that all Christian preaching and teaching—as well as our faith itself—is empty or worthless (*kenos*) without the resurrection of Christ (1 Cor. 15:14). Therefore, on the resurrection of Christ, take your stand and your identity as Christians because the Resurrection is the hinge point of Christianity. Your loving Christ is with you through the Holy Spirit even in your most intense testing and chaos. Trust in him!

In concluding this letter, I pray for each of you, your children, and all of God's children in Christ that you will: (1) always remember what it means to be a Christian, (2) remain faithful to the leading of Christ through the Spirit, (3) never put God or Jesus to shame, and (4) live with confidence that the Lord Jesus is at your side as your present and ultimate refuge—especially in times of crisis.

Love,
Dad / Dr. B.

Questions for Reflection

- Did you expect to find the best biblical definition for a Christian to be in the Book of Hebrews and especially in the context of the severe warning of chapter 6?
- Do you think that when people become new Christians they should be introduced to the warnings of the Bible? Why or why not?

- What does it mean to you that the image of the anchor is also included in this context?
- Do the multiple warnings in the Book of Hebrews make you fearful? Do you think they are necessary? Do you think the Preacher was balanced in his thinking? How would you have treated the subject?
- What do you think about the way Dr. B. handled "J's" question? Would you have handled it differently? Explain.

Notes

[1] For some of my reflections on the Book of Hebrews, see Gerald L. Borchert, "The Fascinating Sermon Called Hebrews" in *Portraits of Jesus for an Age of Biblical Illiteracy* (Macon, GA: Smyth and Helwys, 2016) , 43-53, and "Hebrews" in *Worship in the New Testament* (St. Louis: Chalice Press, 2008), 176-182.

[2] For my analysis concerning the dating and authorship of Hebrews, see Gerald L. Borchert, "A Superior Book: Hebrews" in *Review and Expositor*, 82 (Summer 1985), 319-332.

[3] See Gerald L. Borchert, *Assurance and Warning* (Nashville: Broadman Press, 1987).

[4] This citation in Hebrews 8:8-12 of Jeremiah 31:31 is the longest quote from the Old Testament in the New Testament, and it is crucial to the Preacher's argument in Hebrews.

Chapter 8

The Christian and the Spirit World

Dear Mark, Tim, and Friends:

We turn next to the issue of the Spirit in the life of a Christian, but before we do so I must address a frequently asked question:

Is there really a spirit world?

Many people in our contemporary age regard any notion of the spirit world to be a hangover from a bygone era and frequently posit that even thoughts of it should be eliminated in this pseudo-sophisticated era when we now anticipate interplanetary space travel. Indeed, some of us can vividly remember when an early Soviet cosmonaut while circling the earth sent back a message to those on *terra firma* that he was then in space and saw no god/God "up here."

In the same vein, as we fly in jumbo jets and look down on the earth from 35,000 feet, we may wonder about the relevance of a story in the Bible concerning people building a tower of Babel to reach God and prove that humans are equal to or perhaps superior to God. And if we have not taken time to think about the purpose of that story in Genesis 11:1-9, we may wonder if it is not just an amusing tale from the past. But maybe if we with our sophisticated post-Copernican, space-travel mindsets stop and ponder a little more, we might learn a few things from an ancient writer who never even thought it was possible to fly in a jet from one place to another or encircle the earth in a space capsule.

It has been fascinating to observe during the 1920s, 30s, and into the beginning of the 40s how biblical scholars in Europe were writing a great deal about demythologizing the spirit world in the stories of the Bible. But then it has been very enlightening to observe that in the post-Hitler era, books began to emerge in Europe that dealt with "principalities and powers" in the New

Testament. It was almost as though a few scholars were admitting that maybe the Bible did know a little about the unseen world of the spirit that they had overlooked. Perhaps they realized that they may not have fully comprehended the amazing strength of evil that had been unleashed on the world, particularly from the very country that was instrumental in the birth of the Protestant Reformation.

What does the New Testament have to say about the spirit world?

I invite you to consider this Jesus who was engaged in a battle with Satan or the devil and his forces of evil. That enemy in the Gospel of John is identified as "the ruler of this world," who in the work of Jesus is said to have been defeated, cast out, or defanged (John 12:31)—even though his final punishment awaits the *eschaton* (the end of time). All three Synoptic Gospels give witness to the fact that, even from the beginning of his ministry, Jesus was tempted by the devil/Satan (Mark 1:12-13, Matt. 4:1-11, Luke 4:1-13). And the latter two writers provide examples to indicate how the devil even employed Scripture in an effort to try and sway Jesus from his sense of God's will. John also indicates that Jesus recognized that the devil was behind the attitudes and actions of the self-righteous religious leaders (John 8:44) and in the betrayal of Jesus by Judas (13:2).

But Jesus was not merely aware that the spirit world contained enemies; he also knew the spiritual forces that supported him. When one of the disciples (Peter) tried to intervene in the arrest of Jesus and attacked a representative of the high priest with a sword, Jesus stopped him and informed him that his puny sword could hardly be compared to the force of twelve legions of angels who stood ready to defend the Son of God, if it would be necessary (Matt. 26:53; cf. John 18:11-12).

The Apostle Paul was also clearly aware of the spirit world. Even in his earliest work, Galatians, he recognizes that behind the bondages of humans in this world, there stand the elemental spirits of the universe (Gal. 4:9). In his subsequent letters, he expresses gratitude that the tempter has not succeeded in derailing his Thessalonian converts who are standing firm for the Lord (1 Thess. 3:5), and he warns them to remain alert and put on the armor of faith, love, and hope in their battle for salvation (1 Thess. 5:8-9). Then, in writing to the Colossians as a prisoner who is contemplating the possibility of his forthcoming death, Paul reminds those Christians whom he has never met that in the battle Christ has disarmed the principalities and powers so that the ultimate victory has already been achieved for them (Col. 3:15). In response, he charges them to abandon the meaningless ways of the world because with Christ they have already died to the elemental spirits of the universe (3:20-23).

With this brief introduction to the spirit world in the New Testament, I turn to this question:

Can the Bible help us differentiate between the spirit world and human constructs such as taboos?

I believe that the Apostle Paul in his first letter to the Corinthians sets out two patterns of response for Christians in dealing with such issues concerning the spirit world.

The first pattern is found in 1 Corinthians 8:1-13 where Paul outlines his confrontation with the Corinthian "wise guys." These rebels think they can manipulate Paul in their understanding of what is forbidden (taboo), but they are terribly wrong. They argue that since idols are nothing, it should be no sin to eat meat offered to idols. In response, Paul agrees with them that an idol has no actual existence and therefore its effect on food is nothing (8:4), and that food itself is not a decisive issue when it comes to God's approval of humans (8:8). But that is where the agreement ends; the approach that one has to others concerning their perceptions in matters of faith is crucial.

Idol worship was a reality in Paul's day, and people who believed in the reality of idols were in grave danger of judgment by God—and those who were tampering with the gospel and the destinies of other people were in even greater danger. Paul's response, therefore, focuses on the well-being of spiritually weak persons in their midst. He concludes that if eating meat offered to idols makes another person stumble and lose faith in the work of Christ, he will not eat such meat (8:13). Paul's concern is for others, not himself.

The second pattern is presented in 1 Corinthians 10:14-22 and concerns the reality of the demonic. While Paul would clearly deny the existence of dumb idols, he would never assert that demons or Satan do not exist. Indeed, he knows that Jesus opposed the forces of the devil/Satan and their impact on humans (cf. Matt. 12:28, 16:23; John 13:27). That is the reason Paul warns Christians against attempting to "drink the cup of the Lord and the cup of demons" in his discussion on worshipping at pagan shrines and of trying also to participate in the Lord's Supper (1 Cor. 10:21). With these two patterns in mind, I will now turn to several of my experiences to illustrate these patterns of taboo and the spirit world.

The first example will no doubt cause you to smirk or shake your head in disbelief, but it was serious at the time. I was the junior faculty member and had been teaching at the seminary for a couple of years. Near graduation time, a group of very bright but slightly rebellious seniors (who later became leaders in the denomination) came to my office and told me they wanted to give the school the gift of a pool table for the fellowship hall—because, as they argued, the school needed more recreational facilities.

I responded, "OK, but did you tell the president of your idea?" They asserted quite vehemently that they had done so and that he was shocked: he told them that such a gift would not be appropriate. They then said that they became increasingly disappointed because they were just trying to provide recreational facilities for the students and if the president would not accept their gift, they would never give another penny to the school. That statement got his attention! After listening to their anger, I suggested that they should just pause because I was sure something would work out. Well, the president called a special faculty meeting because the students' potential gift might alienate the constituency.

Now, I knew that my dad had grown up with the view that "a pool hall is a place where the devil hangs out," but he was open to being enlightened and I was sure the president was likeminded as long as he was sure that people would not think the seminary was "going to the devil!" After our long meeting, the president proposed that he would accept the gift, if the students would agree to call the gift the supplying of "recreational equipment." Moreover, he promised to provide a new room where the recreational equipment would be housed rather than in the fellowship hall. That proposition satisfied the students.

Everything passed without incident at the graduation, and then it was time for the trustee meeting. The president waited to see what would happen. The trustees discovered the pool room, and several of them even used it. To the president's relief, all seemed to be acceptable with the trustees. Then he was on a visit to the West Coast where the chairman of the trustees lived. While staying in the trustee's home, he learned that the chariman had a pool table in his basement. When the president returned from that visit, the pool table came down into the fellowship hall of the seminary, and the pool room was turned into a special seminar room for teaching. This experience of taboo concerning the pool table fortunately was terminated without great consequence, but it provided some important insights about the nature of community taboos.

Now, why did I tell this story? It is because sometimes we live with unnecessary "taboos" because of old theories that were based on false presuppositions. But such a response does not mean that something real did not give birth to those taboos. In the case of pool tables, a previous generation linked them with the idea of pool halls that were considered to be poor environments for young people to visit because those who frequented them were often regarded as "seedy." Caring parents wanted their children to be protected from evil influences. For them, pool halls were regarded as "off-limit" places. The same was true for people who regarded playing cards as off-limit because of its association with gambling or who thought of dancing as inappropriate contact with the opposite sex among teens. It also reminds me that when televisions first came on the market, some well-meaning preachers proclaimed them to be "devil boxes." But like all items and patterns of conduct that find their way into our lives and homes, it depends on how our stuff is used and how we live in relation to our calling as servants of God.

I will also remind you that Halloween, which precedes All Saints Day, was thought to be the day when evil spirits had their fling and masks were important so as not to be spotted by the witches and goblins if one ventured out at night. We could ask: Was just one night allotted for the roaming of evil spirits? Of course not! As the biblical writer asserts, "The devil prowls . . . seeking to devour someone" (1 Pet. 5:8).

But that idea leads me to the flip side of the issue and reminds me of the times when I spoke at youth gatherings years ago. Several young Christian college women came to me with questions concerning lipstick. At first I thought they were concerned about the legitimacy of wearing lipstick, but it turned out they were worried that the "hippie" girls were not wearing lipstick and that the hippies had infringed on their symbol of faithfulness to God— and they might be identified as hippies. It seems silly now, but I asked them what they thought they gained by *not* wearing lipstick. They thought it was a symbol of their commitment to Jesus. Taboos can also be status symbols, and the reason we do or not do something can be crucial to us. For young people especially, taboos can be a confusing issue—for example, having tattoos or guys wearing earrings (and indeed on what side one wears them).

Now the second experience I will share was quite different from the above taboos. It took place between what I might, for ease of designation, call a Juju priest and a Christian congregation in an unnamed country of Africa where I was serving as a missionary at the time. It was an encounter that could easily have come straight out of the thinking of Mark, the writer of our earliest gospel. The setting was one in which the Christian congregation had constructed a lovely mud-floor, thatched-roof, wood-benched church at the top of a hill overlooking the nearby village. It was a serene location that could be seen from a good distance, and it served as a fine symbol for Christians in that area. As often happens in such an African context, however, the rainy season arrived with a vengeance and it was virtually impossible for the Christians to get up to their church on one Sunday morning. So when the rains let up a little, the people decided to hold their prayer and witness service in the town square, complete with their joyous singing and their talking drums. It was a heartwarming experience and ended on an uplifting note of praise.

Not much occurred until later in the week when the Juju priest gathered his devotees from the town for their regular meeting with the spirit world. But when he tried to rouse the spirits in his usual pattern, he was absolutely frustrated because, try as he might, the spirits would not be roused to do his bidding. We contemporary Westerners might offer logical, sociological, and possible political reasons why the Juju priest could not raise the spirits. But he was convinced that the plot of ground where he usually practiced his arts had been contaminated by the Christian worshippers, and the Christians were just as convinced that their worship had definitely affected his power to raise the spirits.

So, again, why do I mention this story? It is because I think many of us today do not believe in such a reality as this spirit world encounter. Perhaps it is because we can manufacture various spirit-like experiences with drugs or mimic psychic experiences through psychological manipulation. But the result is that, without reflection, we tend to demythologize all such phenomena as human constructs, hoaxes, or experiences of unenlightened and unsophisticated primitive people. Yet is that answer really adequate?

How should Christians live in relation to the spirit world and the Holy Spirit?

Based on my time spent in Africa and the Caribbean and from my study of Scripture, our contemporary rationalizations concerning the spirit world may be a basic reason why many Christians in the Western world do not take seriously the power of the Holy Spirit in their lives. After talking with scores of Christians, I sense that living with God is more like an idea of being attached to a set of rules or principles for life rather than as a pattern of walking with

God. But God is not a mere book of rules or a set of words on stone tablets. God is a person—however that may be perceived in our theological jargon. And God deals with us in the realm of the spirit and in person-to-person relationships in which we come to recognize that there are powerful realities that impinge upon us that cannot be dismissed or explained easily. These spiritual realities need to be encountered with the authority and presence of God.

Yet it is not easy to discuss such mystery because God cannot be trapped in a test tube or entered into a computer program. While God may communicate with us in various ways, God remains outside of our physical and psychological analyses. But the Creator of the universe is still present in our lives and sometimes spooks us into recognizing this spiritual or even divine reality when we try to discount it. And that presence—which was made known to humans most clearly in Jesus—reminds us not to forget about the spirit world and the eternal battle that is waged between good and evil.

The ancient Mesopotamians sought to represent this battle by the two equal deities of Ahura Mazda and Ahriman that continually wrestled with being in charge. But the great spiritual battle, as the Bible proclaims, is not waged between equal forces. God the Creator, the son Jesus, and the powerful Holy Spirit are not on same plane with Satan, the forces of evil, or the Juju spirits. Although the Bible does not say that humans on their own will be able to resist the devil and the demonic forces in the world, they can do so with the power of God, the "Almighty" one (the *pantocreator* of Rev. 1:8).

Yes, humans who are rightly aligned with Christ can successfully face the powers of evil because nothing in all creation will be able to separate them from the love of God that is in Christ Jesus (Rom. 8:39). And yes, I believe the "spirit" world is real, even though many Westerners may regard such discussions as weird or primitive. The views of the ancients or of current Third World tribes who take the spirit world seriously and seek to appease those spirits obviously do not mesh with many of our contemporary views and presuppositions. Yet while we may think such people are foolish, they still point to a reality that humans do not always recognize. But Christians who have experienced the presence of the Holy Spirit in their lives can bear witness to the fact that the spirit world is an important unseen reality, and such is not simply a theological idea or a confessional statement. While I have sought to analyze my own experiences of the Spirit, they always remain rather mysterious.

One experience may suffice to illustrate this idea. I was speaking at a Christian college along with the famed Dutch heroine, Corrie Ten Boom. On the night prior to the program, the president of the college gathered a representative group of students and faculty members for dinner with the two speakers. It was a very relaxing and pleasant time and as we closed, he asked if we could join hands around the room for prayer and then sing "There's a sweet, sweet spirit in this place." Although I had many times followed a similar practice at such events, it was very different that night as I held the hand of that dear lady who had suffered incarceration at the hands of the Nazis. As we sang, it was like an electric shock hit me and I knew again that God was in that place. I asked others who were present, and they agreed. A wonderful sense of clarity came to me that evening as I prepared to discuss the Bible and science the next day.

Since that time whenever I sing "Sweet, Sweet Spirit," a sense of the presence of God comes to me. Now I realize this could easily be viewed as just my feelings, but I know that God periodically gives me such reminders to indicate that the divine presence is with me. And I pray that you also may have such reminders— some of which may even startle you.

Finally, Jesus indicated that the heavenly Father would give the Holy Spirit to those who ask (Luke 11:13). Moreover, John in his gospel outlines for his readers five significant roles that the Holy Spirit (the *Paraclete*—counselor, advocate, comforter, companion, etc.) has in the lives of believers. In chapters 14–16, as I have detailed in my commentary,[1] John defines these important roles:

- The Holy Spirit will be a constant companion within believers on behalf of Jesus (14:15-18).
- The Paraclete will teach and bring to the mind of believers what Jesus wanted them to know and give them a sense of peace (14:26-27).
- The Counselor will bear witness to Jesus and keep believers from falling (*skandalizein*, in Greek) or becoming a scandal (15:26–16:1).
- The Advocate will use believers to confront others in the world with their sin, with the righteous standards of God, and with the condemnation of the disobedient along with the devil (16:7-11).
- The Spirit of Truth will guide believers and will glorify Jesus by declaring the truth to them (16:13-14).

To conclude this segment on the spirit world, I would remind you that God has given the Holy Spirit to believers to assist us in living within God's created order that has been blessed by Almighty God but that is also troubled by false and chaotic elements—including alien spirits and the evil one that seek to disrupt God's good creation. It has been a standing promise of God to give this Spirit that represents Jesus to humanity in order to provide a divine companionship to Christians for facing not only their daily tasks in life but also for pursuing their God-given commission of making disciples in Christ among all nations throughout our created context (Matt. 28:19-20). This Spirit in a mysterious and unexplained way enfolds the Triune God and is our powerful resource for dealing with the temptations and wiles of the devil. Trust only in that Triune resource for all of life.

In the power of God,
Dad / Dr. B.

Questions for Reflection

- Do you live with any "taboos" in your faith community? If so, what are they?
- What comes to your mind when people talk about "the spirit world"?
- Do you recognize the reality of the spirit world in your faith community? In your own life? How can it be identified in words and beyond words?
- What does the Holy Spirit mean in your life? How would you explain the presence of the Holy Spirit? Can you give any examples of experiencing the Holy Spirit in your life?
- Do you think that Paul and the early Christians understood the spirit world differently than we do today? If so, how?

Note

[1]For my extended discussion on these texts concerning the role of the Holy Spirit, see Gerald L. Borchert, John 12–21 in vol. 25B, *The New American Commentary* (Nashville: Broadman & Holman, 2002), 119-137, 158-171. You may also find Craig S. Keener's works on this subject of the Spirit to be helpful. See *The Gospel of John: A Commentary* (Grand Rapids: Baker, 2003), particularly at 951-970; and *Spirit Hermeneutics: Reading Scripture in Light of Pentecost* (Grand Rapids: Eerdmans, 2016).

Chapter 9

The Will of God and Christian Freedom

Dear Mark, Tim, and Friends:

I turn now to consider the perplexing idea of the will of God.

What do we mean by the will of God or God's will?

The will of God is an incredibly difficult subject to handle because the expression is used quite loosely by many Christians who assume that as fallible humans we can readily infer the divine mind. While we may be able to understand a good deal concerning God's will in general, especially because of the model of Jesus, specifics concerning how God relates to our personal lives are much more difficult to grasp. Nevertheless, it is important for us as Christians to wrestle with this idea because it concerns how we actually view God as a person (*persona*) who seeks to be in a person-to-person relationship with us as humans. It also involves to what extent we really consider that God may or may not lead in our lives and direct our actions as we live on Planet Earth. With this general introduction, let me divide the question into various segments.

Does our view of prophecy impact our understanding of the will of God?

In reflecting briefly on this topic of prophecy in the Old Testament, we must focus on the aspect of "foretelling" rather than "forth-telling"—since both are generally understood to be within the designation of prophecy. The Israelites raised this question concerning how they could determine the legitimacy of a prophecy from the Lord. They found a response in the Torah: "if the word [of the prophet] does not come to pass," then "the prophet has spoken without [God's] authorization" (Deut. 18:21-22). Our contemporary reaction to such an answer would probably be: "Big Deal! That is not much help." And our reaction would be magnified because, in a few chapters earlier we read that if a prophet tells us that something will take place and it does but then tells us to "worship other gods . . . do not listen" (Deut. 13:1-3).

I am sure that on first reading, these texts may seem a little confusing. Yet, there may be some guidance here because the Bible affirms that God does give insights for human activity concerning the divine will. But there are boundaries to any forthcoming insights because, to be legitimate, those revelations must fall within the true nature of who God is and how God acts. But those texts also remind us that God is present and making an impact upon us. Yet, there is also a negative force we have repeatedly called chaos, error, or evil (including the evil one). Furthermore, our presupposition is that chaos is not God's will since God seeks to bring order out of chaos. But for most Christians, these statements miss the basic human concern because people are not primarily focused on obtaining general theological conclusions. So the question becomes:

Can we obtain personal directions concerning the will of God?

Let me respond to this question by providing several accounts of my experiences and adding some reflections on them. The major issue for most Christians with the will of God involves gaining answers to such life questions as: Who should I marry, and what is the best job for me? Followers of Jesus genuinely desire divine insight prior to making their life commitments. Yet the answers to their questions often seem to be a vague mixture of "Yes," "Partly," or "No." Such a confused response is not what we, as mortals, want to hear. We want fixed answers to life's problems *beforehand.* Sometimes we might get what we want, but we might not be ready for what the answer will be at any particular time. And oftentimes we do not even understand the implications of our own questions. Sometimes it takes a little time even to understand ourselves and our relation to our own questions.

When I was much younger and studying law at the University of Alberta in Canada, I started looking for a spouse but was fairly sure of the direction of my life's vocation. I asked many questions of the Lord, of other people, and naturally of myself—whether the person I was dating was the correct one. Little did I know that I would soon leave Alberta for a seminary in Philadelphia and enter a very different vocation. Moreover, the woman I would ultimately marry would not even enter that seminary until a year after I had arrived there. But when she arrived, I sensed almost immediately that she would be absolutely perfect for me. Yet it took her a year to realize that I would be right for her.

As humans we rarely have the capacity and foreknowledge to understand our own questions and receive the answers we seek from God. But our task as Christians is that we should commit ourselves to a life that remains open and in touch with God so that we can recognize the answers when they are offered to us.

But there is a further element to the issue of personal direction that should be obvious in the question of marriage. Since marriage involves two people with their own separate wills, those wills must be aligned or brought together for an effective marriage to occur. My wife will tell you that I sensed the leading of God and was ready to marry her before she sensed that same affirmation and was ready to marry me. Patience, however, is not generally a human virtue.

Then the question often arises among young people whether there is only one person who will mesh well with them. The answer should probably be rather nuanced—such as: "*Perhaps*, in a given time and setting." The more important issue is for couples to discover that under God their fitness for each other can grow and harmonize over time, particularly as they begin to recognize new ways of supporting each other in their common life together. Unfortunately, many couples today do not take the time or energy/effort to build their lives together, and as a result they often grow further apart.

In contrast to the previous illustration, the story of gaining my first full-time teaching position provides a very different paradigm and can suggest a different kind of answer to our question concerning the will of God. We were living in Princeton and Doris, then my dear wife, was teaching in a school some twenty miles away. I had just finished taking my comprehensive exams and was busy beginning my dissertation when it snowed about two feet over the weekend. I was feeling a little ill, so I bid my wife farewell on Monday morning and climbed back into bed to try and sleep off my cold. About mid-morning a telephone call came from the secretary in the doctoral office indicating that the president of a seminary had just dropped in to see if there were any Baptist doctoral students in the biblical field who might be available. To say the least, that call was a surprise. I asked the secretary if I could meet him after lunch, and she said yes. So, I just put on my clothes over my "pjs" and went to the meeting, not thinking too much would come of it.

When we met, the president told me he was staying with his brother in New York and was scheduled to fly to Boston and visit Harvard and other schools there but his flight was canceled because of the snowstorm. His brother suggested that he ought to take the train to Princeton, and so he showed up unscheduled. After talking to him for about two and a half hours, he invited me to come to the seminary in Sioux Falls, South Dakota, at spring break because he was sure the faculty would want me to join them. When my wife came home, she asked me how I was feeling. I responded: "Well, pretty good—I think I just got a job!" That was, of course, a shock. When I told some of my fellow doctoral students the story, they could hardly believe it. I responded, "I guess God must have worked it out because of the snowstorm." Then one of them asked me a stunning question: "Does God care for you more than us?" That appropriate question was a clear rebuke to my naive statement.

I did not know how to answer that question adequately. But the experience was very spooky for me: a snowstorm, cancelled flights, a brother's suggestion for using the train, my status in having finished my class work and ready to write my dissertation, the seminary president needing a New Testament professor almost immediately . . . What should I say?

Some people would brush off experiences of this kind as pure chance happenings and would dismiss any idea that God was in this mysterious combination of events. But while I have no proof, I will still respond by telling anyone: With "eyes of faith," I have seen God in the event. Yet how could I describe it in the vast implications of the world?

Yale professor Paul Minear titled his excellent theological study on the New Testament *Eyes of Faith*—which I believe suggests that even though one cannot really explain the acts of God, the coming of Jesus or divine mystery, people with "eyes of faith" can understand what I am here suggesting concerning God's acting in the course of human lives. Well, I am sure the next question is:

Does God really act in individual lives?

I would continue my response by asserting that I believe God acts and has been in various aspects of my life. But I would be quick to add that my experiences are not programmable because I do not really know how, when, or why God acts in our particular circumstances. But that God acts is, for me, beyond question. Indeed, in this secular culture, I may be considered one of those strange religious people who actually believes in the power of prayer. And I confess: "Yes, I do!" First, I believe that God uses prayer to change me. And then I believe that God often uses my concern and those of others to bring about some changes external to us—which I do not fully understand.

One memory may suffice to illustrate where I am on this issue. I recall vividly a time when I visited a very sick, beloved missionary in the hospital. It was near the closing time for visitors, and I earnestly prayed that God would touch her and heal her. The doctors had been baffled by her condition and were not sure she would make it out of the hospital. But while I was praying for her, a peace suddenly came to me that I should go home because she would soon be well. I thanked God for that answer and left the hospital. The next morning the doctors were astonished that she was much better. In two days, she was released. Yet that kind of healing does not happen often for me. I am sure that it was not just me who was praying for her, but God gave me an answer at a very strategic time. Now, of course, I have prayed for others including my own mother who did not make it out of the hospital but "went to be with Jesus."

So, I would not claim to have the power of healing the sick. Jesus did and the early apostles apparently did, but I am satisfied that I can pray and sometimes be given answers. But I assert that the healing power resides in God, not in me. And I am ready to thank God for how and when it happens. And besides thanking God for healing, I thank God for all the medical personnel who work so hard to help people with their illnesses, and I am exceedingly grateful for the discoveries of new procedures and new medicines. Yet I also firmly believe that God does heal when Christians fervently pray for others. But it is beyond me to predict when and how it will happen beforehand.

Humans cannot program God. Nevertheless, God does hear our prayers. And, while to others it may seem like pure chance that any healing takes place, I am convinced that healing sometimes takes place in orderly patterns but also at other times it is mysterious. We as Christians should be grateful for both regular patterns of healing and those that are mysterious, because all healing is ultimately a wonderful gift to those who are ill.

Why do some relationships not work out, and how does the human will impact the will of God?

Now it is time to turn to the bewildering question of the failure of relationships for those who seek a life partner "until death do us part." I will mention this issue again when I discuss the question of divorce and remarriage, but for now let me consider fractured relationships. Fortunately or unfortunately, humans have their own wills and God has never removed from humans the freedom to choose. So, how do we explain people who believe that it was the will of God for them to be joined in marriage and later become convinced that it was a mistake?

The answer to this question lies in the fact that people are neither static nor are they pre-programmed robots. While God may be faithful and consistent, that quality does not belong to humans. Over time, people change: some couples seem to become more like each other, while others seem to diverge from each other. Likewise, some people who were faithful Christians choose to turn their backs not only on former friends, colleagues, and spouses but also on God.

Freedom is a two-way street that can lead people in different directions. Therefore, do not be surprised by people who change their alignments. They may do so because of a profit motive, by meeting new people who turn their interests in a different direction, by learning new skills, by being influenced by new situations, by experiencing trauma or persecution, by rejecting what was once assumed to be their basic goals or standards, or simply by being bored and ready for a change—any change—to name only a few reasons. Those near to such people, however, may be shocked at the changes—especially the very radical ones. But human freedom comes with a high potential for self-gratification, self-enhancement, and even self-destruction!

Sometimes change leads in a positive direction that includes a growing sense of mature reliance on God, but sometimes it leads otherwise. Change is inevitable, just as growth through the various stages of life can be assumed. But abandoning basic commitments to a spouse or to God in the changing pattern of life can be unusually difficult to accept for others related to such a person. This freedom to change is one reason why the popular slogan "once saved always saved" is a pathetic fallacy. It is built on an erroneous presupposition that humans do not have freedom. Strangely, proponents of this fallacy may allow people the freedom to choose to become Christians but then deny them the freedom to turn their backs on God. But God has not revoked human freedom. Yet God expects humans to be responsible for their actions.

One experience comes to my mind at this point. It involved a well-known, highly educated pastor who was caught being unfaithful to his wife. The church fired him as soon as they discovered his situation. Then the leaders of the church called me to fly into their city each week to serve as their temporary interim pastor while they sought a more permanent replacement.

While I was making those trips, I decided to call the former pastor and invite him to have an early breakfast with me. When he came into the restaurant, his first words to me were: "Jerry, I have to tell you that my wife no longer was fulfilling to me." It was almost like hearing the man (Adam) saying to God "I heard the sound of you in the garden, and I was afraid, because I was naked, and I hid myself" (Gen. 3:10).

Although I had completed several years of doctoral studies in counseling in addition to my biblical studies, this situation was not the usual type for gentle counseling. So after a brief pause, I looked at the pastor and asked him: "Friend, what do you do with sin?" When he recovered from my response, we started to talk seriously about the impact of his actions upon his ministry, the congregation, and especially on the young people who had regarded him as a Christian model. God gave him freedom, but he squandered it in the name of self-gratification and he would have to bear the responsibility for his actions. While God in Christ is in the business of forgiveness, that forgiveness requires many other matters such as acknowledgment of sin, reconciliation where possible, and a commitment to abandon unworthy patterns of living.

These last statements bring up the important issue of taking responsibility for one's actions that seems troubling to many young adults today who have become disenchanted with some of church's rather harsh commitments to firm distinctions between the saved and the unsaved. Since many contemporary young adults tend to be tolerant and open-minded, they wrestle with the thought of God being closed-minded and limiting with respect to those who the church would categorize as "lost" or "not saved." Their commitment to the way of kindness and acceptance is commendable, but these young adults need help in understanding how commitment fits into the stages of salvation.

Locked-in categories do not work for many young adults, especially when they see some people who say they are "the saved" yet act in very unkind ways. They innately know that salvation is a much more complex picture than the instantaneous walking down the aisle that is often presented as the way evangelicals assume one attains the "status" of a Christian. They often sense that not all who profess that status are destined for heaven.[1]

Recognizing the aspect of human freedom in any discussion of the will of God is crucial because it means that our human perceptions of God's relationship to humans must incorporate the tentativeness and fallibility of the human will. Christians may be correct in one or more of their perceptions concerning God's desire for them, but the human mind is still fallible, changeable, and often unprepared to recognize the true nature of God's actions. This conclusion leads to another question:

How does our view of Jesus relate to the will of God and our human actions?

While we cannot enter an adequate equation for God and the divine will into our computers, my reflections and thoughts about the will of God are not fruitless speculations or foolish thoughts because God did provide us with a model for understanding how God's will works for humans. That model is Jesus, God's only Son.

The evangelist John repeatedly sought to identify how Jesus was sensitive to and obedient to the leading of God while on earth. Statements such as "the Son does nothing on his own authority" (John 5:19); "I do nothing on my own, but say only what the Father taught me . . . . I always do what pleases him" (8:28-29); "the works I do in my Father's name bear witness to me" (10:25); and "Father . . . glorify your Son that the Son may glorify you" (17:1) all bear witness to the dependence of Jesus upon his Father, God.

We might argue that since Jesus was divine, he ought to have been able to represent God perfectly here on earth. But since we are only human and are fallible, we cannot expect to be in touch with God as was Jesus. Admittedly Jesus is different from other humans, but the fact is, as Paul says, Jesus emptied himself of much of that divine power and died in one of the cruelest deaths a human could endure in order to be a true model for us (Phil. 2:7-9). He had to be authentically human for us to recognize and accept this gift to us as our Savior, and that is the reason why the incarnation is so important to our Christian theology. That is also the reason why:

- Matthew indicates that Jesus was actually born of a woman in a place called Bethlehem as "God with us"—*Emmanuel* (Matt. 1:23, 2:6).
- Luke tells us that Jesus' birth was very unusual since the virgin Mary conceived through the Holy Spirit and was proclaimed as the Son of God, the Savior, Christ the Lord (Luke 1:27, 35; 2:11).
- John states that the divine Word actually became flesh and took up residence among humans (John 1:1, 14).
- The writer to the Hebrews asserts that Jesus, the Son of God, was tested/ tempted in all the ways we are, yet he did not sin (Heb. 4:14-15)

When the early church fathers reviewed the options concerning the temptations of Jesus (Matt. 4:1-11, Luke 4:1-13, Mark1:12-13), they came to an agreement that the best way to describe Jesus was to say that he was both fully human and fully divine (as indicated in the Nicene Creed). But what did that mean in terms of Jesus' temptations? Three options were open to those early scholars of the church. Using the Latin words *posse* (able) and *peccare* (to sin), they concluded:

1. *non posse non peccare* (not able not to sin)
2. *non posse peccare* (not able to sin)
3. *posse non peccare* (able not to sin)

Option one applies to humans because the Bible tells us that we are all sinners—except for Jesus (Rom. 3:23, Heb. 4:15). Option two cannot apply to us because we do sin; and it should not apply to Jesus because, if it did, it would mean that the coming of Jesus was a mere game and that his temptations were not real. Therefore, option three must apply to Jesus because he could have sinned but did not. I have given you this three-point exercise because it has usually clarified for my students the real nature of Jesus and that he actually faced the temptations that come to us—with one exception. Jesus was not tempted to go further into sin, which means there was no past sin to hinder him from following the will of God.

While we Christians, as humans, continue to sin, we have an authentic model in Jesus of what integrity is like, what love is like, and what doing the will of God is like. This model was neither selfish nor self-centered. As a model, Jesus wished no one ill but cared for the weak, the hungry, the thirsty, widows, orphans, those involved in conflict, those in prison, and those who were mourning (Matt. 5:1-12). Indeed, this model even sought out those who were proud, those who thought they were righteous, and those who had earthly power. But often they were not ready to accept his advice (11:22-45). Yet to those who listened to Jesus and were ready to obey, he gave them the privilege to become the children of God (John 1:12).

There is no question that God is concerned and cares for humans, the pinnacle of the creation, just as the Lord cares for all of creation. Moreover, God cares about how humans relate to the rest of creation because they are stewards of the creation. But God has a special concern for how we as humans relate to one another, as Jesus made quite clear in the Sermon on the Mount (Matt. 5:1–7:29). But while the Lord cares for us and commends us to throw our anxieties on our Creator and Redeemer (1 Pet. 5:7), God does not force us to conform to the divine will.

Instead, God is like the father of both "prodigal sons." The one was self-oriented, traveled where his money would take him, and sought to fulfill his human desires in what the Bible calls the desires of the flesh. The other (the stay-at-home brother) was like the self-righteous Pharisees and scribes whom Jesus was addressing and who was just as demeaning of his father while condemning his wanton brother. The Lord waits patiently for both types of erring children. God longs for some of us to return from our self-centered journeys away into unseemly areas of distraction and seeks for others of us to turn from our self-righteous attempts to criticize others while protecting our status-quo views that we are the measure of divine acceptability (Luke15:11-32). Whoever we may be and whatever we may be doing, our God keeps calling us to follow the model of Jesus and become conformed to the image of his Son (Rom. 8:29).

How does Paul encapsulate for us the model of Jesus in living out the will of God?

God does not will for us to become automatons in order to do the divine bidding. But in freedom, God wants us to choose wisely and listen attentively to the inner promptings of the Holy Spirit who can even help us pray when we do not have the right words to utter and when we can only sigh that God's will may be done (Rom. 8:26). Paul knew that all of life involves choices and that our choices impact not only ourselves but also other people. Those choices can even affect the destinies of people yet unborn, so we must take care and accept our responsibilities as we make choices so that they may be wise. For a wonderful summation of what the Christlike life should be, Paul's appeal in Romans 12:1 to 15:13 can be for us an encapsulation of the will of God.

To be authentic representatives of the will of God (12:2), Paul expects Christians to be "living sacrifices"—evidencing transformed minds that direct the entire functioning of our lives ("bodies") for the purpose of service/worship of Christ (12:1). These sacrifices are not just dead or inanimate offerings, but they actually require the commitment of a person's full selfhood. Thus, thinking, doing, and being are all combined in this concept of the will of God. Moreover, the Christian is not merely an individual in isolation. Rather, Paul views each Christian as an integral part of Christ's body—the church—and each one is expected to exercise any God-given endowment(s) for the benefit of the whole community of faith (12:3-8). This symbolism is amazingly holistic and is a challenge to the individualism and narcissism of our times.

With this composite image in mind, Paul then spells out how the will of God should be perceived first in terms of interpersonal relationships. In keeping with his view that growing in the sanctified life is identified with the Christian characteristic of love, he begins his list of Christlike actions with loving others and then he moves through such qualities as serving the Lord, rejoicing, being patient, giving to the needy, blessing others, living in harmony, not being conceited, overcoming evil, etc. (12:9-21). He follows this list by focusing on matters of public life: respecting government rules and requirements such as paying taxes (13:1-7; cf. the model of Jesus in Mark 12:13-17 and parallels).

Paul's goal, like that of Jesus, is not mere obedience to rules and regulations but to love others. Moreover, the overarching significance of love is the basis for his Christian interpretation of the second ledger of the Decalogue (Ten Commandments) in Exodus 20 (Rom. 13:8-10). And he summons his Christian readers to wake up and abandon the ways of darkness and debauchery and to live in the light of the coming ultimate day of salvation (13:11-14). Paul concludes this extended appeal by advising Christians to avoid judging and condemning others who set up unnecessary and picky religious requirements over food and worship as patterns of piety and obedience, because walking in the love of Christ does not place stumbling blocks in the way of others who seek to relate to God (14:1-23). Respecting the weaknesses of others and helping them to discover and glorify the God and Father of our Lord Jesus Christ is for Paul his foundational understanding of God's will and of Paul's own purpose in life (15:1-13).

Even though we live in a context that can be frustrating, unclear, and chaotic and despite the fact that we are frail and sinful and often do not make the best choices, we are still called to face life with the confident assurance that God will be with us, that the Lord Jesus truly loves us and that we can lean heavily upon the Holy Spirit for divine guidance. In closing this discussion on the will of God, therefore, I pray that the Lord may be with you as you seek to live boldly and authentically as deliberate Christians. Do not fear: God is with you in your journey. But earnestly make it your commitment to follow the promptings of the gracious Holy Spirit as you make your choices and decisions in the name and in the pattern of our Lord Jesus Christ, who is the authentic model for your life.

Cordially,
Dad / Dr. B.

Questions for Reflection

- Why do you think the Israelites were looking for clues to whether a prophecy was true or false? Why do Christians look for clues to understand the will of God?

- Have you experienced mystery in your life? How have you tried to explain it?

- Have you experienced any negative changes in people that are difficult to explain and accept? Without naming names, can you describe those negative changes? Do you think that human freedom has played any part in those changes? What about positive changes? Do you think that freedom had any part in those changes?

- Do you know any young adults who are wrestling with other people being lost or condemned? How do you approach them? Do you think that Dr. B.'s explanation concerning the stages of salvation might help any of them? Explain.

- What does the concept of "eyes of faith" mean to you?

- How does the model of Jesus assist you in understanding the will of God? Why do you think the New Testament writers went to such lengths to explain that Jesus was both truly God and truly human?

- Why you think Dr. B. considers the Beatitudes in Matthew 5:2-12 to be crucial in helping Christians to understand and do the will of God?

- Why do you think that, even though we as humans are weak and frail, Dr. B. has advised his sons and readers to live boldly and authentically in the name of Jesus?

Note

[1]When it comes to entering the blessed state of heaven, I recommend that those who are wrestling with the misunderstood issue of exclusion should read the fascinating book by C.S. Lewis, *The Great Divorce*, for a suggested way to understand why some people do not enter the heavenly state (a bus ride to heaven)—namely, as a self-determining action by a person.

Chapter 10

Divorce and Remarriage

Dear Mark, Tim, and Friends:

Having briefly mentioned the issues of marriage and divorce in other sections, including the previous chapter on the will of God, I turn now to address specifically the question of divorce and remarriage that has troubled Christians for ages. Let me begin by asking:

What is the church's problem with divorce and remarriage?

While I have been confronted with the issue of divorce and remarriage a number of times, perhaps an experience I will share from a trip I led to Israel may help you understand my perspective. Then after I quote to you from a letter, I will comment on what I think is the biblical perspective. But before I detail this encounter, let me set the stage with a few preliminary reflections from my early life that may give you some additional insights into my approach on this matter.

When I was growing up, experiences of divorce and remarriage were rare and many wonderful Christians from my church in Canada looked at divorce as the result not merely of failing the marriage vows but as something akin to a stigma that irreparably marked a person as some special sinner. I remember asking my dad why Mr. E., a senior member in our church and a very loving Christian, was not a deacon. Dad responded that Mr. E. had been divorced and was remarried. As a result, Mr. E. did not consider it permissible according to the Bible for him to be an officer of the church. That statement stuck in my mind because it seemed to me at the time that divorce must be almost like having committed some unpardonable sin.

For centuries divorce in the church carried a terrible stigma because marriage was regarded as indissoluble, especially if a wedding was performed in a church. It was an "until death do us part" event. So, how could divorce be accepted by the church? Unfortunately for the church, theological declarations do not always represent human realities. What then should be done?

We can change such theological declarations to conform to reality, or we can pretend to change reality. For hundreds of years the church chose the latter option if one could pay for an official declaration that the marriage should be regarded as null and void—it was a convenient mythological means for dealing with the church's demeaning problem. The partners were absolved of any guilt of having been wed in the first place, and they could remarry without any concern for breaking church rules. While such a solution may appeal to some and is a practice in some denominations of the church, it is just a game that fails to face the human reality of divorce squarely. Divorce is a tragedy! Dreams, plans, and promises have not been realized. But it is not the end.

In reflecting on my earlier experience and the game some people play, I turn now to reflect on my experiences as a minister of Jesus Christ. I have faced this issue of divorce a number of times, including the question of hiring one of the premier evangelical New Testament scholars when I was the dean in a seminary. I again would assert that divorce is a tragedy because previous hopes and dreams have been crushed and vows to God and the church have been broken. Moreover, I would add that from my experience—even though it may be difficult to admit—there is no point in playing a blame game and asking who is responsible for the divorce or who is the so-called guilty party. We are all sinners and are responsible for how we live and acknowledge our sins before the living God.

But I will try to explain later why, from my perspective, divorce is not an unpardonable sin. I am convinced that God does not hold grudges but is willing to forgive us and enable us to rebuild our broken lives. Forgiveness and the challenge to move forward is the message of the gospel. It is the perspective that Jesus proclaimed in dealing with repentant people and those like the woman accused of adultery by the Jewish religious authorities. Jesus told her he would not condemn her and that she could go but not to repeat the sin (John 7:53–8:11).

What can we learn from this serious response of a divorced person?

Here is an excerpt from a very telling handwritten letter I received from a woman who went on one of my tours to Israel:

Dear Dr. Borchert,

I am sure you won't remember me, but you lectured on our bus in the Holy Land . . . . I had almost made up my mind to skip the evening lecture, but you helped me in what you said. I want to say thank you. Why? Because you made me feel like a human being after all!

I grew up in an orphanage, married my high school sweetheart, and I thought it was for life . . . . It was a nightmare, but I gave him chance after chance and after 3 children and 5 ½ years, I was only a mere 82 pounds. I got a divorce . . . . there was such a stigma to it, and most people thought I was a failure. I wasn't a Christian . . . . I started going to church . . . . I met [his name] . . . I said I would join the . . . Church. I was baptized at 29, and it truly was a life-changing experience . . . .

Whenever the topic of divorce came up, it was very difficult and so judgmental. I attended a life-and-work conference and a minister there asked if anyone was divorced. I hesitated and then I admitted I was. He said, "Well, I would never have married you!"

Because of my divorce, people always looked down . . . . and think they really didn't try to make it work . . . . Then you came along and gave me a new perspective. You said that divorced people can still be useful in the church . . . . I could finally let those unkind thoughts of other people float away . . . .

[Signed] _____

This letter says it better than I can. First, let me remind you that you never know when you can be a messenger for God in Christ—even when you are traveling away from home! Second, the letter reminds us that pharisaic-type people are still living and present in the church today—and we must take care that we will not be one of them. But, third, my perspective on this issue grows not only out of a desire to follow the pattern of Jesus, but it also emanates from a little research into the biblical view of divorce that I think has been badly misunderstood by the church.

What insights on divorce can we gain from the Old Testament?

The place to begin thinking about divorce is the Old Testament, where Moses gives the concept of a divorce document to women as a symbol of liberty in a patriarchal society.[1] In the culture of Moses' day, women (and children until the age of maturity) were basically regarded as possessions of their husbands (or fathers) and were subject to their demands. The divorce document freed women from continuing to be the possession of ruthless husbands who had usually abused them and put them out of the house. Those women were thus forced to fend for themselves while still being the possessions of their husbands. Then, in the event the women were able to gain desirable goods, money, and property, the husbands could still take possession of such property from the wives they had dismissed. Such women were usually consigned to serving as mistresses for men who desired sexual pleasures (see the very pertinent example in the story of Tamar in Genesis 38; contrast Hosea and Gomer in Hosea 1–3). Divorce became the merciful basis for giving freedom and a new life to those women who had been badly abused and abandoned.

But remember what Deuteronomy 24:1-4 tells us: "When a man takes a wife and marries her, if she then finds no favor in his eyes because he has found some indecency in her, and he writes her a bill of divorcement and puts it in her hand and sends her out of his house and if she becomes another man's wife . . . . her former husband . . . may not take her again to be his wife . . . ."

While this Scripture seems to treat the woman as having few rights, the point is that a woman may have prospered and if she gained wealth from someone, the original husband could not legitimately take over the property she had inherited or had come to possess. This text assumes the man's right to put his wife out of the house, but the bill of divorce was an early expression of giving women personal rights.

How is divorce handled in the New Testament?

We must be careful in reading the Greek text of the New Testament. In Matthew 19, the Pharisees ask Jesus what cause is legitimate for putting away a wife. This questions does not mean (as many translations suggest) that the man is divorcing his wife. The questioners are trying to involve Jesus in the age-old rabbinic argument over a man's rights in dealing with his wife in matters of indecency—"putting away a wife," as reflected in the above Deuteronomic text. The answer is hardly what the men want to hear because Jesus reminds them that the husband and wife became one. Moreover, it is probably a blow to the male ego when Jesus reminds them that a man is said to leave father and mother and be joined to the wife—not the reverse (Matt. 19:5; cf. Gen. 2:24). But then the questioners push the issue further and asked about the divorce document. Jesus' response is no less unsettling for them when he tells them that Moses gave the document because of the hard-heartedness of men: the point was that men had difficulty living with their wives (Matt. 19:7-8).

If this answer is not enough, the disciples add to the discussion by suggesting like spoiled children that if such were the case, it would probably be better not to get married. Jesus' response to them is basically "Take it or leave it, boys! The Kingdom's ways are different than the ways of the world" (19:10-12). There is little doubt that for Jesus the separation of a husband from a wife is a tragedy. Such was not God's intention. But was such a separation for Jesus an unpardonable matter, as was so often regarded in the history of the church? I hardly think this conclusion is the case.

Can the Hebrew terms and discussions help us in dealing with divorce?

One of the basic problems in the history of the church is that it has confused divorce with what was regarded in the ancient world as a man's almost-sovereign right to dismiss or "put away" his wife. While it was hardly God's intention that husbands and wives should separate, the church has confused "putting away" (*shalach*, in Hebrew) with the more gracious Mosaic concept of a wife receiving a liberating certificate of divorce (*keriythuwth*, in Hebrew). But the problem has been exacerbated by the fact that English translators have frequently rendered the Hebrew *shalach* as "divorce." Thus, God says in Malachi that "putting away"—not divorcing—the wife of your youth is an example of Israel's faithlessness to God (Mal. 2:14-16) and God is tired of Israel's injustice (2:17). In Jeremiah 3:8, however, the word *keriythuwth* is used and God is said to be divorcing (giving a certificate of divorce to) Israel because of its unfaithfulness. God then faces this question: Since Israel has been handed a certificate of divorce that normally is final (Jer. 3:1-5), should or could God take her back (3:6-10)? God, of course, can handle that problem.

Now, here is the crucial point: "putting away" or dismissing a wife and "taking another" does not in the Old Testament mean that the man has divorced his wife. That is the problem with many translations on this issue. Jesus undoubtedly understood this rabbinic distinction and critiqued all such patterns of meanness and loose morals.

Yet the brief text in the Greek of Luke 16:18 creates a slight problem because out of the blue and without any contextual framework the verse charges all divorced persons who remarry with adultery. Did Luke understand the Hebrew distinction? I do not know. The context of the woman taken in adultery in John 8 reminds us of the way Jewish men handled such issues since only the woman was brought before Jesus and charged by the Jewish leaders, indicating that men seemed to be above criticism.

But the matter of marriage in the Old Testament is further complicated: marrying a second or more wives did not mean the man had committed adultery (consider, for example, the patriarchs—Abraham and Jacob—and David). The pattern of marrying multiple wives is seemingly not condemned in the Old Testament. Accordingly, we must conclude that women were not regarded as equals with men in biblical times. Thankfully that pattern has been moving in a more positive direction today.

Even in New Testament times the text of 1 Timothy 3:2 and 12, where bishops and deacons are admonished to be the husband of one wife, reminds us that Roman society was also rather cavalier on this issue and it was not unusual for a man to have more than one wife—and he may have had mistresses in addition to his wife/wives. It is Christianity that has given the world a transforming perspective on marriage as well as on racial, economic, and sexual differences (cf. Gal. 3:28). Unfortunately, not all Christians have been in the vanguard of such crucial societal changes. But we can be thankful for those visionaries who continue to lead in the caring mission of building a better society where humans are recognized as equals and as created by God, thus deserving not to be treated as second-class citizens.

How should Christians respond to the concerns over divorce and remarriage?

I would conclude by asking that you make every effort to treat women and men as equals and that in this era of the chaotic, mushrooming divorce rate that you treat kindly those who have experienced the tragedy of a marriage dissolution. And pray for the children who have experienced the divorce of their parents. They may not even understand how deep their need may be for support and understanding. Divorce is painful and leaves deep scars on people that are not easily healed. And even in a new marriage those scars will persist and the newly married couple and their children will live with those scars for life.

Divorce in society is a reminder that this world is not a utopia. Our utopia awaits the new heaven and the new earth when all will be changed. In the meantime, remind your own children that as they contemplate marriage it takes love, commitment, prayer, and a reliance on God to build a marriage in which two people are truly joined in Christ. The Lord Jesus came to make evident God's grace to all of us, and we are called to follow his model of self-giving love.

In Christ's love,
Dad / Dr. B.

Questions for Reflection

- Do you know personally any people who were divorced? Have they shared with you any feelings they have experienced? Without naming names, can you share any of those feelings?
- How does your faith community handle the marriage of divorced people? Are they treated as equals in the membership? Explain.
- Is your Christian fellowship freely able to discuss concerns about marriage? Do you have a marriage enrichment class in your fellowship? What subjects are discussed?
- Are men and women treated as full equals in your church/fellowship? Name issues that indicate they are treated as equals and issues in which they are not treated as equals.
- What could you and your church do to help divorced people feel completely welcomed and accepted?

Note

[1]See Gerald L. Borchert, "1 Corinthians 7:15 and the Church's Historic Misunderstanding of Divorce and Remarriage," *Review and Expositor*, 96:1 (Winter 1999), 125-29.

Chapter 11

Homosexuality

Dear Mark, Tim, and Friends:

Homosexuality is a hot-button issue today. It is not an easy subject to talk about because it involves hostile political views, staunchly-held theological positions, and great emotional sensitivities, in addition to dealing with personal and/or physical aspects of people for whom Christ died. So:

How should we approach such a divisive subject as homosexuality?[1]

Let me begin by assuring you that the issue of homosexuality is not merely an academic one that has gained my attention. It has been thrust upon me as an administrator, a minister, a professor, and a trustee. I have encountered a number of situations in which I have been asked, even challenged, to give my opinion about people whose careers and even the well-being of their lives was at stake. And I have needed wisdom far beyond my own to begin dealing with such situations or giving even a modicum of advice on this very sensitive question of homosexuality—an issue that is currently ripping churches apart.

Sometimes it behooves us to pause and remain silent, but that is not possible in all situations. Nevertheless, we are called by God to be people who are known for integrity, people who are to model love and harmony, people who are expected to protect the weak, and people who seek to build bridges between troubled humans. Sometimes it is necessary for us to take an uncomfortable stand between opposing views and to suffer attacks from both sides in an effort to be a mediating voice in the midst of hostility and outright conflict.

Self-confident people who assume they can speak for God concerning the lives of others can be among our greatest challenges—and I must admit that I have not always been free of such patterns during my life and ministry. Unfortunately, in some of the discussions on sexuality I have encountered Christians on both sides who have reminded me of being like the religious leaders who thought they had the mind of God as they dealt with the blind man in John 9. But those religious leaders had to learn from Jesus that they were actually the ones who were blind. Such self-confidence can also arise among Christians who are confident that they have the mind of Christ in terms of their social and biblical understanding of freedom.

We live in a narcissistic, "me-centered" society that eschews rules and misunderstands liberty. Some people are convinced that old community rules and customs are inherently unfair, antiquated, or illogical. Both types can be unbending in advocating their views and determined that the other side is devoid of the correct understanding of the Bible and reality. Both can march for their views and prompt others to respond negatively, sometimes perhaps in violence. It takes considerable wisdom, therefore, to deal with those who have become radicalized in their positions and whose beliefs and emotions have become so interlaced in their particular commitments that there is little room left for allowing opposing opinions. My concern here is that we should be as Christlike as possible in dealing with others, especially those who suffer rejection when they seek to live before God honorably.

Of course, there are other humans who believe they can do whatever they want. But true freedom implies taking responsibility for our actions. Flouting sexual permissiveness, such as I witnessed at the gay parade when I was teaching in San Francisco, is not my concern in this message to you. But that parade brings up the issue of societal rules. Every society has rules concerning what is appropriate, and people can react in a number of ways to those rules. Hopefully, people's reactions will be appropriate in the social context and Christians will seek to walk humbly and circumspectly with God in newness of life—evidencing the various aspects or fruit of the Spirit such as love, patience, kindness, gentleness, and self-control (Gal. 5: 6-22).

So, if you keep Paul's idea of walking with the Spirit in mind, let me turn to the Old Testament texts concerning the divisive subject of homosexuality.

What does the Old Testament have to say about homosexuality?

The two texts that are the most relevant to our discussion concerning homosexuality come from Leviticus 18:22 and 20:13. The first text appears in a series of one-verse prohibitions beginning with "You shall not . . .," and it continues with "lie with a man as with a woman" because it is "an abominable sin." The second text, appearing in a series of conditional sentences, is even more specific: "If a man lies with a man as with a woman, both of them have committed an abominable sin; they shall be put to death and their blood is upon them." There is no doubt from these texts that a sexual relationship between two men is regarded in this Holiness Code of Leviticus as a capital offense, punishable by death. Women are not included here because their status is not really free.

The Holiness Code, initiated within Israel after the escape from Egypt, was designed to give Israel an identity as a holy people who belong only to the Lord God (*YHWH*). These people are to be different in both morals and worship patterns from those in the surrounding nations and particularly from the Canaanites into whose land they are settling. That is also the reason sexual morality issues appear in the same context as the proscriptions against the worship of Molech (Lev. 18:21, 20:2-3) and against turning to wizards and mediums for spiritual guidance (20:6). The people of Israel are clearly called to consecrate themselves as a holy people because the Lord alone is to be their God (20:7).

In this Holiness Code, as is typical of the Old Testament, men are viewed as superior to women. The laws are not gender neutral! Sons count; daughters are mere additions. As in succeeding generations when the synagogues were formed, ten men are required for community worship. Women can worship (often in a separate section), but they do not count in the ten. The mere thought of a man being penetrated is regarded as a major disgrace. (In the ancient world, conquerors often humbled losing warriors as a means of proclaiming victory over those who were defeated.)

What insights can be gained from the ancient camp hospitality codes for the story of Sodom?

We turn now to the story of the destruction of Sodom and Gomorrah, which is usually regarded as disgusting to contemporary Western minds, but is frequently mentioned in connection with homosexuality. In reflecting on this story, readers need to understand ancient Near Eastern cultural patterns and the concept of the camp. Those inside the camp were duty-bound to protect the camp at all costs. Those outside the camp were viewed as potential enemies.

The Hebrew greeting *Shalom* and the related Arabic word *Salaam* hark back to the idea that a traveler who was passing a camp should be welcomed, be given clearance to enter, and should experience protection and "peace"— not hostility. Such a visitor should in principle then be given something to eat or drink as a gesture on the part of the host to provide assurance of welcome and of protection by the host in the camp for a limited period of time. These gestures were part of the ancient code of hospitality to travelers in desert areas where those outside the camp—especially at night—could be subjected to all sorts of threats and even death from animals, the elements, and marauders. The host, then, was bound by the code to protect the traveler while in his tent or house.

But not all camps or communities were welcoming to strangers, especially if the travelers were part of a huge crowd that threatened to overwhelm the camp while the travelers were en route to their destination—like the crowd of traveling Israelites who were part of the exodus from Egypt. Those Israelites discovered as they traveled through the desert areas on their way to the Promised Land that they were not welcomed. As they encountered hostility, they were frequently forced to do battle to gain passage through the lands of those who were settled there.

Understanding this code of travelers provides readers with a clearer basis for interpreting both the story of Lot protecting his visitors by offering his daughters to be raped in Sodom (Gen. 19:1-29) and the equally revolting story of the Levite who chopped up his dead, raped concubine and sent pieces of her to the tribes of Israel as a call for them to avenge his honor (Judg. 19:1–20:11, esp. 19:29-30). Note: these stories are not about consenting homosexual activity but about how the ancients treated unwanted visitors. Raping a man was a means of humbling him, and such was the repeated practice of conquering armies in dealing with their conquered foes.

The point of these two stories in Genesis and Judges is virtually the same. Judgment should fall on those who fail to observe the code of hospitality in welcoming travelers. By this statement, unlike the two texts from Leviticus, I mean that these stories neither approve nor deny consensual homosexual activity. It does, however, mean that humbling a man by raping him was an outrage. Yet, offering women to be raped in order to protect male visitors seems to have been less outrageous a practice, since women were regarded as inferior to men. But as I stated in my letter on divorce, we can be very thankful that such views concerning women have been slowly changing.

In further reflection on this matter, it is interesting to note that while Sodom is certainly regarded as a symbol of a wicked city that deserved the judgment of God, with the exception of adultery and wantonness that are linked with Sodom in Jeremiah 23:14 and Ezekiel 16:46-56, there are no references in the Old Testament that even closely link the city to homosexuality (cf. for example, Deut. 29:23, 32:32; Isa. 1:9-11, 3:9-10; Jer. 49:18, 50:40; Lam. 4:6; Amos 4:11; Zeph. 2:9). The same is true concerning Sodom in the

New Testament (cf. Matt. 10:15, 11:23-24; Mark 6:11; Luke 10:12, 17:29; Rom. 9:29; 2 Pet. 2:6; Rev. 11:8) with the exception of the brief statement in Jude 7 that might suggest there were some irregular patterns of sexual activity present in Sodom.

In addition to the vague Old Testament texts on Sodom, what does the New Testament have to say about homosexuality?

You probably expect me to turn to the specific passages in Paul that are often quoted in discussions concerning homosexuality, namely, Romans 1:18-32 and 1 Corinthians 6:9-11.

The Romans passage is set in the context of affirming Paul's great thesis statement concerning the gospel and God's righteousness as the power of God that leads to a saving new life for all (Jew and Gentile) who believe or have living faith (Rom 1:16-17). Paul is fully aware that everyone is a sinner before the righteous God and needs transformation that comes through the sacrificial death of Christ Jesus (3:21-25). And in the last part of Romans 1, Paul details the decadent state of humanity that refuses to honor God and (as a matter of choice) subverts the worship of God (1:18-23). As a result, God consigns humans to suffer the consequences of their choices in three resounding verdicts related to the darkening of their wills, their passions, and their thought processes so that they engage in all sorts of malevolent practices (1:24-32). Detailed among these activities are the unnatural sexual relationships of both men and women (1:26-27).

In the 1 Corinthians passage, Paul is writing to a group of Christians living in Corinth, the new Roman capital of Achaia (southern Greece) reestablished by Julius Caesar at the crossroads of the ancient Mediterranean world. Imagine for a moment yourself in this great cosmopolitan city lying on a narrow isthmus between the Peloponnese and the mainland, a navy town situated between two harbors named for the two supposed sons of Poseidon (the sea god) and known for its loose morals. The sailors enjoy their shore leaves while their ships are loaded and unloaded or pulled across the narrow strip of land on rollers from one shore line to the other.

In this context, the brief text of 1 Corinthians 6:9-11 provides a stern reminder to believers that those who practice the activities of a wicked society "will not inherit the kingdom of God." Then, like the Greek philosophers who enjoy providing lists of vices and virtues, Paul provides his own list. But he is deadly serious with those who are committing condemnable vices. As you read

Paul's list of vices, see if you think they are all of the same weight: the immoral, adulterers, idolaters, drunkards, revelers, thieves, greedy people, and cheaters. Then into that list Paul inserts two words that probably relate to homosexuality (6:9-10). And he adds that "some of you" were so involved, but you have been transformed by Jesus and the Spirit (6:11)!

I think I have reflected accurately on the meanings of these biblical texts to both of you, my sons, who are ordained ministers and who, I am sure, have been pressed by people for quick responses to the issues of homosexuality. But I want you and others to know that the last statement concerning 1 Corinthians 6:11 has given me pause, just as the text of Romans 1 has forced me to ask some lingering questions about homosexuality.

There is little doubt in the meaning of the terms or the activities according to Paul. Moreover, I have no doubt that Scripture is clear concerning the normativity of heterosexual relationships. God created humans as male and female and intended them to live as "suited" for each other in "unashamed" unity (Gen. 2:23-25), but that sense of harmony has been tragically disrupted.

I am still troubled, however, by the issue of choice. The story of the blind man in John 9 remains in my mind and has thrust upon me a further question. When the disciples ask Jesus, "Who sinned that he was born blind?" blindness is not normative. In essence, Jesus responds: "That's the wrong question, boys!" Accordingly:

Could we be asking some wrong questions about the issue of homosexuality?

I wonder if we in the church have been asking some wrong questions and therefore positing some wrong answers. I have no doubt that Paul meant what he was saying about homosexual activity because history tells us that in the Greek world young boys were used by men, including some well-known philosophers. I will not discuss this matter further here, except to say that such patterns are not an approved normative lifestyle for Christians.

Thus, I see a number of perspectives staring me in the face, especially after I have listened to a number of parents who have told me stories about their gay children. The repeated message I have heard is that "as early as I/we can remember, he/she was a little different than our other children." Then a number of years ago I began reading and listening to professional people talking about the genetic ladder and gene therapy. I began to ask myself a series of important questions, including:

Could the genes of a person get cross-wired?

By that question I mean: Could the physical aspects of persons be different from their psychological and social aspects? And then the frustrating question hit me: If it is possible for them to be different, can we determine which is the most determinative for a particular human being?

Since I began asking these questions to myself, the news media has reported on a number of transformative surgeries that have taken place. Perhaps the most shocking one was the surgery on Bruce Jenner. Then the question followed: Why would a robust male, medal-winning athlete want to become a woman? And another disturbing question followed: Are we still in the era where the male is regarded as superior in the subconscious minds of most people? Is the male regarded as more desirable than the female? The disturbing answer came back: In the minds of most people in our enlightened culture, I think the answer still must be "Yes, I guess so."

It was not the answer I wanted because it was the same answer I heard when my wife, a faculty member in the seminary where we were teaching at the time, asked whether the rest of the faculty would support her if she sought ordination in that denomination. I am thankful that the question could be answered differently in another denomination where we taught later. Yet I remind you that even though we may glibly quote Galatians 3:28, does that mean we believe it?

So, what do all these questions imply? What about the original question concerning the possibility of cross-wiring in humans? I think the answer should be that we need to be very careful in rendering judgment about humans in fields where we are not sure we know all the facts. The disciples were sure that someone must have sinned in the story of the blind man. All they wanted to know was whom they could blame—they thought someone must have been guilty of sinning (John 9:2). But they were blissfully mistaken. That kind of seeking to assign blame on someone can still happen to us today.

I still have questions on the subject of homosexuality—perhaps more than I have answers—but I trust that you can sense we need a few more answers before we blame people and render our judgments. One of those questions is:

When we misunderstand the nature of the human self-centered will, how does it factor into our views?

Our view of the human will is evidenced in the open flouting of narcissistic, chosen permissiveness whether among so-called gays who spurn morality or among self-centered straight people—and I can name a few in high office to which such applies, even some in the church! Moreover, there are those who think they know the will of God for others.

For the first, such patterns are completely antithetical to the biblical principles of holiness and the recognition of God's standards in relation to the demands for purity in humanity. It represents the condemned pattern of life that Paul outlined clearly as wicked and the replacing of God, the Creator, by honoring instead the darkened mindset of those who seek meaning to life from sexual pleasure and lusts for power and privilege (Rom. 1:18-32). I would also venture to suggest that it might be evident in the legalistic, pseudo-righteous who do not permit openness to new truth but consider that they possess the final answers to reality and accordingly can judge others.

Both suffer from a similar problem of substituting themselves and their views for the living and dynamic God who not only continues to create but also allows us to discover new realities. Some of the former are willing to admit that they refuse to acknowledge and honor God and the divine demands. The latter usually plead that they are following their understanding of the will of God that is enshrined in time-honored catch-phrases and logically deduced formulas that have for them represented God's will and that they use to hammer others.

But in contrast to both, I would advance the perspective that we should not dismiss the imperatives in the Bible as irrelevant to our contemporary world setting. Those statements were based on what humans understood at that time about their physical and psychological make-up and the need for humans to relate with integrity to each other. Yet we must ask: Is the biblical view of gender inequality appropriate for Christians today? The answer must be a resounding no. But some members of churches still need to discover this truth. Is the biblical goal for an organized family structure important? The answer should be yes. Is the ancient means for attaining that end appropriate for people and families today? The answer again should be a growing no. The patriarchal family model is definitely flawed.

Did the biblical writers perceive the possibility that people could be cross-wired in their physical and psychological constructions at birth?

I sincerely doubt it. We are just beginning to wrestle with this possibility. Should we as Christians be open to recognize the possibility that such differences might exist in sincere believers in Christ? This is the burning question that today is dividing many churches. Some will argue that such cross-wiring is impossible and people should be subjected to affirming only their physical features. Somehow, I suspect that such an answer may someday soon prove to be incomplete and inadequate. And the issue becomes more difficult when we ask questions concerning the meaning of marriage and far more difficult when we posit scores of questions related to church membership. If for the present we are unable to wrestle with these questions, some day they will be forced upon us because of the information explosion that is taking place. Exactly what that information will reveal concerning humanity and the full implications is still hidden, but glimpses of their meaning and import are on the horizon.

Are Christians open to the information explosion?

I would suggest that the church of the Lord Jesus should remain open to receiving new insights into truth about the nature of humanity and how the biblical message can be related to new insights. When I was attending law school many years ago, I learned that the half-life of an engineer was ten years. In other words, half of the information an engineer would need to know in ten years was not yet available, discovered, or developed. I am sure that the time period has since been shortened considerably.

Several examples should suffice here. First, in 2018 when Warren Nielsen and his team of medical students at the Health and Science University of Portland opened the cadaver of 99-year-old Rose Marie Bentley, they were stunned to find that her organs were reversed. Yet she lived a perfectly healthy life and we would not have known that such a phenomenon was possible without her donating her body to research.

Second, the C-Pack (cortisone) has been almost a wonder drug for bringing rapid healing to many people. Yet for some adults it has caused great harm to their neurological and brain functions, often taking medical personnel by surprise and leaving loved ones asking questions of "why?"

Third, we have learned a great deal about dementia, but the more medical treatments we develop, the more variations of the disease seem to emerge. As individuals, we are continuing to gain new answers to enhance our understanding of our body and especially about how our brain functions.

My question remains: Are the church and individual Christians prepared to deal with new information that becomes available, or are we stuck in the past and its condemnations? Do we really care about people and their frailties as much as our own? I am not advocating that frailties are normative, but I am suggesting that we must be very careful in rendering our condemnations.

I am confident that the biblical message of Jesus as our Savior and Lord will be as relevant in the future as it was in the days of the early disciples, but are our churches and ministers ready to engage the new information that is bombarding us daily? That is the unanswered question.

What might be some helpful advice for Christians on the issue of homosexuality?

Without denying the normativity of heterosexual relations in Scripture, let me suggest the following:

- We need to be honest that many Christians do not fully understand the physiological, psychological, and sociological issues involving why some people are or at least seem to have different sexual orientations than their physical features.
- We need to treat everyone with the graciousness of a true follower of Jesus and not condemn people when we as Christians might not be certain of why people react the way they do.
- We need to support parents who wrestle with loving their children when they do not understand the way their children think or act.
- We need to be gracious to those who believe their gender orientation is not what we think it should be.
- We should be ready to support those who wrestle with their own selfhood as children of God who constantly stand in need of God's love and forgiveness and God's power to overcome human weaknesses as they attempt to live authentic lives before the Lord and the world.
- We should pray for clarity both for ourselves and for those who think differently than we do, asking God to give all of us the ability to treat each other with understanding and love in spite of our differences.

Some churches not only welcome but also affirm those who claim a different gender pattern than is usually understood and accepted in society. Some churches will clearly not accept such affirmations. This difference is more than obvious. But I pray that our continuing differences will not lead to further church wars and splits and that we will sometime soon be able to find sufficient grace with God's help as humans to accept one another for who we are as people created by God with all our human differences, foibles, and failures. Along these lines, the Methodist Church tried to reach a type of accepting pattern in February of 2019. Some constituents were pleased with the divided vote that affirmed a firm traditional approach, but others were saddened that the same vote rejected an accepting-divided pattern for their general conference. Such problems and decisions do not die easily. They have a way of living beyond themselves and haunting the future.

New models for dealing with this issue will certainly continue to emerge and be proposed in the future among various denominations, and they may or may not cause a further fracturing of the body of Christ. Yet as new and more authentic medical and social information becomes available, we may learn how to handle the issue with more grace. But until then, we may have to remain with some sense of continuing differences of opinion and a sense of chaos between how people interpret both society and the Bible. But maybe we can learn to be more gracious. I wonder: How would Jesus handle these issues?

Are you ready to deal with the confusion and chaos? Are you prepared for what lies ahead? You will need the wisdom of God as you seek to be authentic messengers of Christ in proclaiming both grace and salvation to the generation that lies before you. I challenge you: Try to get prepared for what is yet to come. To be prepared, you will have to place yourselves in the hands of the living Christ and seek to follow where the Lord leads you. Remember that the future of the church still has to be written. You will be part of that script, so write carefully!

In Christian hope and love,
Dad / Dr. B.

Questions for Reflection

- What do you think Dr. B. means when he talks about "gender neutral"? How important is it? Is your church/fellowship gender neutral?
- How does the historical understanding of the camp code and welcoming strangers impact the way you interpret the story of Lot, his daughters, and the visitors to Sodom?
- Do you think it is possible for a person's genes to be cross-wired? If so, how would that affect your understanding of homosexuality? What do you think about the Bruce Jenner story?

• Is your church open to receiving new insights from science concerning the nature of the human person?

• As you reflect on your church/Christian community, who do you think might be your church's unpardonable sinners today?

Note

[1]For a detailed discussion of homosexuality, consult Robert A.J. Gagnon, *The Bible and Homosexual Practice: Texts and Hermeneutics* (Nashville: Abingdon, 2001).

Chapter 12

Confronting the Dark Side and the Reality of Evil

Dear Mark, Tim, and Friends:

Throughout our study we have been reflecting on the presence of chaos in the world and how it has affected almost every aspect of our human reality. We began with chaos and worked our way through issues of equality, integrity, Christian infighting, political realities, the spirit world, freedom and the will of both humans and God, divorce and remarriage, and homosexuality. We have also briefly reflected on victory in Christ and his role in our salvation and what it means to be a Christian in terms of the significance of our ethics or actions. Before we move to the subjects of death, heaven, eternity, Christian worship, and pertinent current and future ethical issues, we need to address the serious issue concerning the Dark Side and the reality of evil in the world. Let us begin by asking a question:

Why is there evil in the world when the Bible says God is good?

Unfortunately, the Bible does not answer some of the most basic questions concerning evil, nor does it answer the question concerning the origin of evil. Yet it has been evident to humans from the beginning of time that there is not only chaos but also a dark side that we call evil in this world. The question of why a good God would allow evil in the created reality, however, is hidden in the mystery of God and creation. As a result, humans have sought in various ways to answer this question throughout the ages. Indeed, I have often told my students that if they could solve the question of the origin of evil, they would be billionaires or more. And they would probably control the world—if God would allow them to do so!

The seer in the Book of Revelation hints at an answer to the question of evil when John pictures the embodiment of the Dark Side in the form of a superhuman entity, not quite divine (note the mixture of the numbers 7 and

10 indicating confusion; Rev. 12:3), who is identified as a dragon. This dragon has repeatedly sought to frustrate God's will and to eliminate God's messianic answer from the world. While the dragon did succeed in killing Jesus through the combined power of Jewish and Roman political maneuvering, it could not succeed in canceling the work of God's Messiah, because Jesus was raised from the dead and was caught up into heaven (12:3-7).

This dragon was then cast down to earth—not by God but by Michael, a subordinate servant-warrior of God. In frustration at not being almighty and unable to reverse God's plan in the world, the dragon has continually sought to destroy, confuse, or at least gain a foothold among God's people. While the dragon may be able by its clever wiles to gain many human adherents and even a number of "Christians" through temptation and/or persecution, John boldly asserts that it will not ultimately succeed in its devilish attempts because God can use even the earth to prevent such a victory (12:8-17). So, the next question that must be raised concerns the actions of Jesus in this superhuman struggle, namely:

How do the temptations of Jesus help provide understanding for our confrontations with the devil and the powers of evil?

In the temptation stories (cf. Matt. 4:1-10, Luke 4:1-12) Jesus is portrayed as unmasking the ways of the Dark Side. The Gospels demonstrate through Jesus how the tempter can and does use any means in its attempts to deter, frustrate, and derail Gods' people in their goal of living in the world according to the ways of God's goodness, truth, and righteousness. Humans can easily become confused and misled by the evil intentions of the devil, and can succumb to the wiles of the tempter unless they are very alert and rely on God.

Clearly, in these temptation stories the "precise" words of Scripture are not paramount in obedience to God and authenticity of life. Instead, it is the "intentions" of God in the words of Scripture that are the defining factors. Anyone—including the devil—can use the words of Scripture for evil purposes, and even Christians have done so in the course of history. But Jesus showed through his encounter with the devil that understanding the intentions of God in Scripture is critical for God's people. Scripture is not God! But Scripture can lead us to God under the guidance of the Holy Spirit. Make no mistake about this difference! Many people who thought they were being faithful to God have misused Scripture and in doing so have succumbed to the Dark Side or the wiles of the devil, including determined Jewish rabbis in the days of Jesus and Christian priests, ministers, and lay people in succeeding generations.

Remember: the serpent misled the man and the woman in the garden by simply changing the command of God into a question (Gen. 3:1), and the devil used scriptural texts with Jesus to assert God's divine support and protection of him, even if he would not follow God's will (Matt. 4:3, 6; Luke 4 10-11). But in both cases the devil's goals were contrary to the intentions of God.

Lying can be very subtle, and the devil is a master at lying. Indeed, in the Gospel of John, as Jesus is criticizing the religious leaders for being children of the devil, he details that the very nature of the devil is that of a liar and that his intentions have nothing to do with truth. The devil only uses some elements of truth to twist the truth for his purposes (John 8:44). From that lying nature of the devil come murder and other patterns of evil. And I should add that in today's era of narcissism, snippets of truth can often be employed for the devilish ends of the Dark Side!

The mention of these Jewish leaders in John brings up the next question:

What can we learn from the way Jesus confronted the presence of the Dark Side in humans?

It is easy for us to assume that if anyone's ideas or life patterns do not conform to our perspectives, then the other people must be from the Dark Side. The problem with such an assumption is that we are not God. Nor do we, as humans, have the wisdom and understanding of God or Jesus.

There is no question that Jesus did judge and condemn people such as the religious leaders of his day, but he knew what was in humans and he knew their inner motives (Mark 7:9-23, Matt. 15:6-20). And even though humans were unworthy of his love and sacrifice, he still came to rescue them from the snares of the devil.

His love and care for humans is the reason why Jesus could even allow Judas to be a participant in the strategic foot washing and final supper events, although he knew that Judas had already committed a treasonable act in betraying him to the Jewish leadership (John 13:2). Could Jesus have rescued Judas? The answer seems to be suggested elsewhere in the gospel when it says; "I chose twelve of you, but one of you is a devil" (6:70). Although that response for some could open the wormy can of "reprobation" (negative predestination), it does not mean that Judas was determined to be a devil. Such a suggestion is an argument from silence.

Instead, I would draw your attention to the fascinating probable positioning of the disciples around that great supper table that must have been a *triclinium* (a three-sided U-shaped lounging table where the disciples' feet stretched behind them and, leaning on one elbow, the disciples ate with the other hand and were served from the front side of the table). While it might seem incredible to us, the beloved disciple and Judas likely had the two places of honor at the table: one at the front and one at the back of Jesus. From that reclining position, Jesus easily could dip a morsel in the bowl and hand it to Judas (John 13:25-26).

Think about the pathos at that event: The traitor is present and seemingly positioned next to Jesus when Jesus hands him the morsel of bread. Then Satan takes control of Judas. That is the point of no return, and Jesus commands Judas to leave quickly from his presence and do what is planned (13:27). Then spotlighting the trauma of that event, when Judas departs, John adds: "It was night!" (13:30). The Dark Side is, indeed, closing in. It is not simply a time designation! Evil usually operates under cover, but here evil is unmasked in its ugly, dark strength.

How many of us could have handled Judas in such a scene without either collapsing or striking out in anger? Whenever we are tempted to judge another person, we should remember this portrait of Jesus with Judas. The participants are not sitting around on chairs playing a game or at a table as Leonardo Da Vinci pictured! The disciples are trying to relax and recline in comfort at the beginning of a familiar Passover meal. And, as Mark suggests, they have been through some very exhausting experiences.

The disciples have recently been stunned by Jesus when he informs them that: the Temple will soon be destroyed (Mark 13:2), they will become the subjects of persecution (13:9), and the terrible woes predicted by Daniel will soon come to pass (13:14). The disciples have also witnessed the strange anointing of Jesus, in which they heard him declare that the action is for his burial and that this event will be remembered and is proclaimed around the world into the future (14:8-9). They are ready for a break to celebrate the marvelous hand of God in freeing the people of Israel from Egyptian bondage.

Then it happens! Suddenly, Jesus announces that one of them will betray him. It shatters any sense of tranquility the disciples have anticipated, and each begins to ask: "Is it I?" But instead of simply using the familiar words of

Passover, Jesus breaks the unleavened bread and announces "This is my body." Then he raises the cup and says, "This is my blood of the covenant which is poured out" (Mark 14:22-24).

Everything seems to be changing. Is all hell breaking loose? The answer seems to be yes, especially as they finish the supper and Jesus says: "You all will abandon me!" Peter tries to assert his faithfulness but is promptly told that before the rooster wakes most people, he will deny Jesus three times (Mark 14:27-30). But that is only the beginning. From there, it goes downhill very fast. Jesus takes the disciples to pray in the garden, but they fall asleep. Then the arresting band comes with Judas, who betrays Jesus with a kiss (14:45). But the Johannine evangelist does not give Judas any credit, reminding his readers that Jesus identifies himself with the electric words "I am" after which the arresting guys actually fall helplessly before him. And it is Jesus who instructs them to take him into custody but that they should let the other disciples go free (John 18:1-9).

Do you recognize that John wants everyone to sense that in this story a great superhuman battle is taking place between God and the dark forces of evil? And at almost every point thereafter John seems to paint a picture that humans are not in charge of this supra-historical event. Not only does Jesus not bow to the pressure of the godfather high priest, Annas, and the Sanhedrin in their interrogation. But when one of the attendants slap him, Jesus counters with a retort: "If I have spoken truthfully, why did you strike me?" (18:23). Later, when Pilate asks Jesus if he is the King of the Jews, Jesus responds by asking Pilate if he asks that question on his own authority. That is a shock to the governor, Pilate. But Jesus does answer that he is indeed a king and has been "sent to bear witness to the truth." Pilate then reveals that he is a typical political manipulator when he asks the haunting question, "What is truth?" (18:38).

Yet Pilate does declare that Jesus is innocent and seeks to release him. But when he tries to use a political gimmick to win the people's agreement by giving them the choice of freeing either Jesus or a criminal, they choose the criminal, Barabbas (18:38b-40). Having lost that round, Pilate seeks to placate the mob by having Jesus, the one already declared "innocent," beaten. He then places Jesus on display as a helpless king wearing a crown of thorns. But that ploy to gain their sympathy does not work, and he discovers that Jesus is called the "Son of God." That announcement sends fear tingles down Pilate's spine, and he realizes he is dealing with a far bigger issue than what has appeared on the surface (19:1-8).

So, Pilate moves into a recalculating mode and tries to question Jesus further. But when Jesus refuses to answer, Pilate tries to threaten him with his power. Jesus, however, responds by informing Pilate that he has no power except by divine permissiveness (19:10-11). That answer only convinces Pilate more forcefully that he does not want to get into this high-stakes religious battle. But the Jewish leadership has another evil card to play. As I have often indicated to my students, Pilate's goal in life has been to follow his patron, Sejanus, and be designated a "friend of Caesar." Those conniving Jewish leaders know Pilate's "Achilles" weakness. So, they play their winning card: they will report him as not being a friend of Caesar (19:12)! Pilate loses his gamble and what is left of both his integrity and authority.[1]

The rest of this ugly story is well known concerning the crucifixion of Jesus, but I would remind you of several points of light in this dark battle between God and the forces of evil that the Gospel writers wanted their readers to observe:

- It almost seems that God stepped in and Pilate finally found a backbone with the Jewish leaders when he insisted that the inscription on the cross was to be none other than that Jesus indeed was "The King of the Jews." Moreover, the charge was written in the three major languages of the Roman province of Palestine at that time—Hebrew, Latin, and Greek (John 19:20-22).
- In spite of the furor, Jesus did not neglect his duty to his mother as the eldest son. He was in charge, not his Jewish mother (John 19:26-27; cf. also the wedding feast at 2:4-5).
- Jesus died and gave up his spirit when he chose, not when humans expected him to die. And like a perfect Passover lamb, not a bone of his body was broken in the typical *crucifragium* (breaking the legs to end support for breathing, John 19:30-32).
- The veil to the inner sanctuary of the Temple that separated humans from God was torn from top to bottom, signaling a new opening of the way to God (Mark 15:38; cf. Heb 10:19-20).
- When the Roman centurion who was in charge of the crucifixion witnessed the events of the death of Jesus, including the earthquake that seemed to be related to it, he confessed that the one on the cross truthfully must have been the Son of God (Mark 15:39, Matt. 27:51-54).

• After the soldier pierced Jesus' side, and both water and blood emerged, the witness—probably the disciple—highlighted this fact (John 19:35). This notation probably does not refer merely to some particular physical phenomenon, as some commentators have sought to explain, but more than likely to the promised connection of Jesus' redeeming death to the two great symbolic actions of the Christian church, namely baptism and the supper. (Remember: When reading John, we must recognize that it is filled with symbolism and is not a simple newspaper report.)

Jesus' death was not the end of the story, nor is it the end of the supra-human battle that has been waged between God and the forces of evil. That battle of the cross climaxed in the historical event of the resurrection of Jesus—the most important event in human history. In the Resurrection, God guaranteed that evil would not prevail, that the devil and his dark forces would be defeated, and that in the end "death"—the final enemy (1 Cor. 15:26, Rev 20:14-15)—would be eliminated. The question that follows then must be:

What are the implications of Jesus' resurrection for Christians in the battle with evil?

In John, the Resurrection means the beginning of a new era. The risen Jesus has breathed the Spirit on the disciples (John 20:22), just as God breathed life into the human (Gen. 2:7). The disciples come to realize with Thomas that Jesus is not merely a human messenger from God but is actually their Lord and their God (John 20:28). And the disciples understand that while they have all been cowards like Peter and they all have abandoned their master, yet also like Peter they have been restored and given a divinely ordained mission to the world (18:15-27, 21:15-22).

The mighty power of the Resurrection ushered in a new era, and with this event came some expectations of Christians:

• We are to do all that is humanly possible not to rely upon ourselves but to depend on the insight, wisdom, and strength of God to resist the temptations of the devil (1 Cor. 10:13, Heb 2:18).
• We are to be wise as "serpents," yet as harmless as "doves" (Matt. 10:16) so as not to lead others astray. At the same time, we are to watch out for ourselves to avoid being caught off guard by individuals and situations that reflect the bewitching work of the evil one (Gal. 6:1).

- In our confrontation with evil, we are never to minimize nor misunderstand the immense power of evil and the ability of the devil to confuse humans about the nature of truth and who is the real enemy of God. Rather, we are to seek guidance and wisdom from the Lord, who is the only truly wise resource in the universe (Rom. 11:33-36).
- We must understand that we are not immune to persecution nor spared from trouble, but have a companion in the Holy Spirit who is at our side to keep us from being compromised and scandalized (John 15:18–16:4)—if we place our trust in the Lord.

What insights do the Pauline Letters provide in this battle against the forces of evil?

Although we must be very careful in defining our enemies, Christians can learn something quite significant from the Pauline references to the armor of an ancient warrior in terms of resources for battles against the unseen principalities and powers of the dark world and of the spiritual forces of evil (Eph 6:12).

In his early letter to the Thessalonians, Paul begins to reflect on those battle resources in terms of the triad of salvation—"faith, love, and hope"—when he refers to the breastplate of faith and love and the helmet of salvation, or hope (1 Thess. 5:8). These three characteristics outline for Christians the three stages of salvation.

That brief portrait of the armed Christian warrior is later brilliantly expanded and redesigned in Paul's powerful conclusion to the circular letter of Ephesians (6:14-18) in which the Christian warrior is pictured as armed with a number of items, including:

- The belted covering of "truth": In the battle with evil, Christians must never compromise on the truth (John 16:13). To fail in honesty implies the inviting of chaos and the dark way.
- The upper body armor or breastplate of "righteousness": Integrity and righteousness are basic to God's nature—not ours. In Christ, God's servants have been declared acceptable and righteous. Yet we do not cease to be sinners, so we cannot boast in our own integrity. It is in the integrity of Jesus that we find our basis for righteousness (Rom. 3:21-26) and our ability to battle the forces of evil.

- The spiked shoes of "peace": In the Beatitudes, Jesus indentifies peacemakers as the children of God (Matt. 5:9). Our stability in the battle with evil requires peacemaking, which is different than mere peacekeeping. The latter is what the world seeks among troubled people, but peacemaking requires the quality of love that marks a Christian (John 13:34-35).
- The protective shield of "faith": The Christian understanding of salvation begins with faith and is foundational to all aspects of the Christian life (Rom. 5:1). Trusting in the divine presence in our life and service is the key to overcoming doubt, frustration, hopelessness, and the other attacks of the evil one.
- The plumed helmet of "salvation": Salvation is the ultimate gift of God to humans (e.g. Rom. 6:22-23), but it is not merely futuristic. As we live with God in faith, love, and hope, there a great inner sense of confidence to face the onslaughts of evil and chaos from without.
- The offensive sword of the Spirit, which is the "word of God": The directives of God provide Christians with the means to confront evil in settings that are not only personal but also corporate and public. God does not will for Christians to crawl into a shell and let the world go by. We are expected to influence everything around us because Jesus has sent us on a mission to bring about transforming patterns of life and thought to the world (Matt. 28:18-20).

There is one more element of armor that is often omitted, and I will comment on that element after I reflect on an experience I had as a youth.

As I was reading John Bunyan's famous book, *Pilgrim's Progress*, which my parents gave to me, I came to an abrupt halt in my reading and I have never forgotten that experience. I can still sense my reaction as I read about the fearsome Apollyon facing Christian on the narrow path to his goal of the Holy City. Pilgrim becomes terrified, then stops and is about to turn and run. But he suddenly realizes he will never survive if he does so; he has no armor on his back! If he turns and runs, he will be dead. There is only one way for him to go: forward. He has to do battle with the dreaded evil monster. Can he do it? With everything in him he begins to pray. Then turning fully toward the monster, he marches forward—and he wins the battle.

The last item in the resources of the Christian warrior must be prayer. But it is not a piece of external armament. Prayer is an internal resource—and it is essential! Prayer provides the backbone or the will to engage the Dark Side.

Evil is powerful, but God is more powerful. The Christian warrior needs God not only for strength but also for determination, wisdom, calmness, fortitude, equilibrium, and the gifted qualities of the Spirit (Gal 5:22-23). This battle is not merely against human enemies but against the spiritual powers of the universe.

You may ask if I think most Christians are ready to face the spiritual powers of the universe. I am not sure. But you may also ask me if I think we can actually encounter agents of evil and the Dark Side? Now my answer is an absolute yes.

As I was boarding an airplane one morning and taking my seat after having had a very positive time at worship services the previous day (Sunday), I sat down beside a woman who had on her lap a black covered book and was jotting down some notes on a pad. I thought she was having her morning devotions. When I asked her, she told me: "No, I am not a Christian." She was a Wiccan and was engaged in praying to the Dark Side that ministers would fall to temptation—including those related to the family of Billy Graham.

Since then I have asked several of my classes how they would have handled that situation. Some students had encountered a type of the Dark Side, but most had not. Yet, most understood clearly what is meant by the Dark Side. They have watched space movies! The Dark Side is active today, and Christians had better be prepared with prayer and a strong commitment to the Lord Jesus if they are to be ready for encountering such experiences in the future. God is not weak, but neither is evil. The question is: Are Christians today ready for such encounters?

One of my friends has been doing research on the Hitler era for about twenty years and is ready to publish some of his materials on the German S.S. leaders and the alignments he has discovered concerning Himmler and his colleagues. His stories are chilling! Their commitments to the Dark Side were very evident—including wearing symbols of their attachment to evil. Be alert: evil has its advocates, and they will become more evident in the future. As Christians, we can become tricked by those advocates who continually use lying as their means to confuse people and gain supporters. Jesus knew them. Do we?

But to return to the armor of God, I believe that an unprepared warrior trying to use God's armor might lose the battle. Of course, God could surprise us, as he did in the story of Jonah and the Assyrians—although Jonah refused the results! In the belly of the fish he had prayed, but I often wonder about that prayer. Prayer is essential for humans in their spiritual battles. Humans cannot by themselves conquer the Evil One. Spiritually weak Christians can quote Bible verses *ad nauseam,* but it may have little effect. But Scripture or an idea from God bathed in prayer and living in the mind and heart of a spiritually attentive Christian can champion a reformation!

In conclusion, I welcome and encourage you to join God in this great battle against the evil enemy who delights in chaos and destruction. But please do not neglect prayer! In the midst of chaos you can be envoys of transformation. Yet I forewarn you: The battle against the Dark Side is not easy. Be prepared for opposition and a toll upon your life. Still, you can with Christ's help experience the incredible joy of being agents of a divinely inspired renewal through Christ working in you. Yet I sternly advise you concerning whatever you may accomplish for God: Be sure, as servants of the Lord, that you give the credit and the praise to God in Christ Jesus!

In the spirit of our Lord Jesus,
Dad/ Dr. B.

Questions for Reflection

- Why do you think Dr. B waited until this point to deal with the problem of evil?
- How do you react to the difference between the intention of God and the words of Scripture? Can you think of other ways the devil could use Scripture for evil purposes? Can you think of other good things that could be used for evil?
- What would be your reaction to the discussion of Judas being at the foot washing? At the last supper? What would your reaction be to Judas if you were in the place of Jesus?
- How do you react to the idea that there is a superhuman battle going on in the world? That there was a superhuman battle going on in the life of Jesus? That there is a super-human battle going on in your life?
- How important is the Resurrection in your thinking? In your life? How much do you actually reflect on the Resurrection?
- What have been the most important resources for you in your battle against evil?
- How do you react to the idea that the Gospel of John and the other gospels might be more than just newspaper reports about Jesus?

Note

[1]Pilate never did achieve his goal and finally was removed from office. Moreover, the family members of the high priest were eliminated by the Jews themselves because the Jews blamed the fall of Jerusalem on the manipulations and unfaithfulness of the Jewish people on the high priesthood.

Chapter 13

Death, Heaven, and Eternity

Dear Mark, Tim, and Friends:

If there is any issue that forces us to think beyond our current reality and the way we live, it is our thoughts about death and our future. So, our initial question must be:

How do we as Christians regard death and our resources in this life?

We in the Western world may confess the old adage that there are two things of which we can be sure: death and taxes. But having been a lawyer, I can tell you that most people do not like to think about their death. Indeed, many people postpone writing their wills and testamentary documents as long as possible. In fact, some wait so long that they die intestate, leaving the state to decide on the distribution of their assets—which may not be what the deceased would have desired in terms of beneficiaries and estate taxes.

Hopefully humans will not end their lives thinking that "all was vanity and the chasing after the wind" (Eccl. 2:11). But like a wise person, they will reflect seriously about death and be prepared for its reality (7:4). The Preacher (Qoheleth) reminds us in his conclusion that, in the end, fearing God is the key factor of life and that there will be an accounting in which even the secrets of humans will be revealed (12:14).

These thoughts about death remind me about some intriguing experiences my brother and I had when we were growing up. We both worked for a major cemetery in the city of Calgary, Alberta, during the summers. While we were primarily the kids who cut the grass and occasionally tended the flowers and bushes, we learned a good deal from those who dug the holes for the caskets, especially when the grave diggers dug up an earlier burial to provide space for a newly deceased person who wanted to be buried in the same pit with a loved one. I can hardly forget the day when the grave diggers uncovered a woman who had been down for several decades. Almost all of her body had deteriorated, with the exception of her blond hair, because of the moisture at that place. But when the air and the shovel came in contact with her hair, it almost immediately disintegrated. In a sense, it was there one moment and gone the next!

The form was there, but the materiality had virtually disintegrated. That experience has repeatedly reminded me of Paul's words that what is "sown is perishable, but what is raised is imperishable" (1 Cor. 15:42). We are often so concerned about giving a relative a proper burial, we forget that a corpse knows nothing, feels nothing, and cares nothing about what is left. The person is not there because the persona has departed from the body. Some people fear and argue about whether it is appropriate to cremate the body, but my response is that it will decompose anyway.

The God who created the physical body is perfectly capable of creating an imperishable one. By the way, do not think that it is difficult for God, the Creator, to resurrect a believer who has been burned at the stake or cut up and buried in multiple places or buried at sea or devoured by land or sea creatures or dissolved in acid or eaten by worms. (When my former students and Christian friends in Singapore die, they are cremated because there is not enough land available for them to bury their bodies. That is the reason I told one of our relatives not to worry that his mother was cremated.) Christians have better things to do than worry about the body of a loved one. They should, of course, deal with the body respectfully, but they should also focus on remembering their loved one's life and on using that person's resources to care for those who are still living and in need.

How do we envision a biblical view of heaven and eternity from our context of time and space?

Appropriately, we now turn to the issues concerning heaven and eternity. As I have stated elsewhere, many assumptions are made concerning the biblical texts related to these issues.[1] Hopefully, as a biblical interpreter, this brief review will challenge you to reflect more deeply on some of the most crucial questions you will meet when dealing with people concerning their misunderstood ideas and misguided folk traditions related to heaven, eternity, the soul, and the hereafter. But I must preface my remarks by saying that I have not been to what we call the heavenly state in order to confirm my statements. Yet I have tried to deal in my remarks here by reflecting on a few New Testament texts.

Let me begin by considering a simple example I offer my students concerning God and humans in the context of time and space. I begin with the issue of space because it is the easiest one to comprehend. When I put a chair in front of my students and I sit on it, no one else can sit on the chair, not even my wife—although she can sit on my lap. The reason is that I have occupied that space. Now parenthetically, I know that technically within and between the molecules of a body there is plenty of space present so that I should be able to pour another body into it. But my body will prohibit another body from occupying that space with me. Nevertheless, my Christian teaching informs me that God can occupy that space with me. God can sit on the chair with me because God is not limited by the confines of earthly space.

But that is not all. The same God, who can occupy my space, has the capacity to understand my speech and thoughts in any language or means of communication available to humans. This fact was brought home to me powerfully when I was a young boy and I heard my grandmother pray about me in German. All I understood at that time was my name, but I was wonderfully impressed that God and my parents could understand her. That incident, of course, encouraged me to learn German. But these two illustrations point to the need for us as Christians to think beyond our space and communication boxes. They force us to think multidimensionally.

With these thoughts in mind, I turn to the matter of the interrelationship between space and time because that relationship is crucial for understanding our concerns about death and the resurrection. When most people think about eternity, they basically insert eternity into their framework of time. For example, they may confess that God is beyond time, but they normally view eternity as a continuation of time with a space adjustment.

They usually envisage that in the beginning there was God and time. But what happens when we start to think that God created time and that before the creation, the concept of time did not exist? That kind of thinking often implodes a person's thought processes, especially if one tries to talk about what happens to someone after death. Our thought processes are oriented to time and space. Indeed, even the words *before, when, where, eternity,* and *heaven* imply for us time and space dimensions. But God, heaven, eternity, and the Resurrection cannot be squeezed into those parameters. So, these concepts generally shut down our rational processes. We are generally left to frustrating speculations.

What was the understanding of the afterlife among other cultures such as the Greeks and Egyptians?

Most ancient religions begin their theological reflections on "God" with assumptions about time and space and the creation of their "god(s)." The biblical message, however, assumes the reality of God and posits the creation of time and space. The questions of where God was in the beginning or when God came into existence are not treated in the Bible because that information is beyond human understanding. Nor is the question discussed of how long eternity will last. Eternity is outside of the framework of time. Indeed, the Greeks did not actually have a word for eternity. Their concept of time was cyclical or one of repeating ages (eons, or *aiona* in Greek).

To deal with their questions and frustrations concerning the afterlife, the Greeks posited the concept that an individual or a person was composed of a body and an entombed "soul"—which awaited death in order to escape from its bodily tomb. The question emerged: What would happen when the "soul" was released from its bondage?

The Greeks, like all people, were fully aware of issues regarding justice and fairness, and they understood that they would have to answer for the way they had lived. Their view was that at or after death, the soul of that person (if the person had been just) would ascend into a paradise and be absorbed into the great soul of the universe. If the person had been unproductive, unjust or evil, however, the soul would have to be re-entombed (or reincarnated) into a different body of a lower creature—an animal or a different person (depending on the extent of the injustice or evil). The point was for a creature or a person to escape from its physical bodily tomb and enter its goal of being absorbed into the eternal soul. According to Plato, a philosopher was the most privileged type of a person or creature because a philosopher would understand reality best and therefore would not have to wait and suffer multiple reincarnations before admission to its paradise in the great soul.[2] (In terms of Plato's thinking, that would probably mean my brother, Don, who is a philosopher, should make it to "the great soul" long before I would!)

The view of the Egyptians in the religion of Isis for dealing with justice issues after death, however, seems to have been a little more advanced. In studying my papyrus copy of the judgment scene from an ancient tomb (which comes from the Valley of the Kings and Queens near Luxor), the vivid illustrations based on the Book of the Dead reveal the successive stages of judgment as one moves through the registers. The dead woman in the painting frames from the ancient tomb is assumed to have been properly embalmed and buried. She is then led by her conductor to the judgment hall before eleven judges. These judges are charged with determining whether or not her heart while on earth was lighter than a feather. An executing crocodile waits patiently in anticipation of a tasty meal should she fail in her test of justice. In this example from the tomb, the woman passes the test and is then conducted before Isis who reads a brief summary of her life's history and rewards her in the afterlife according to her good deeds.

Preparation for the afterlife was an important and repeated theme in the history of Egypt, and especially among the pharaohs who gave particular attention to the construction of their tombs (including building pyramids) and to the preparation of their bodies for passing into the next world. But as you can imagine, after my many visits to ancient tombs throughout the Mediterranean world and to countless museums I am left with an indelible impression that elaborate tombs may be magnificent treasuries for grave robbers and archaeologists, but are of little value to those who have died. Once a body stops breathing, a person's possessions are meaningless except as bequests to others.

How did the developing understanding of the Israelites/Jews differ from that of other cultures?

By contrast, the Hebrew people—who came out of paganism—gradually developed a linear concept of time and envisaged God's goal for them to be the entrance into a promised land. But when the "Promised Land" did not prove to be the expected paradise for which they had hoped and they suffered defeat and the trauma of a subsequent exile, they began to realize that their idea of an earthly promised land was hardly adequate and probably represented just a mundane terrestrial representation of an ultimate heavenly destiny (cf. Heb. 9:23-25). That is the point at which many Jews began to deal more intensely with the ultimate issues of time and space. Accordingly, a serious debate ensued between the old rural order of Sadducees and the new urban order of Pharisees over individual responsibility and the emerging understanding of resurrection.[3] Ultimately the Pharisaic view won because the earthbound views of the Sadducees completely collapsed with the destruction of the Temple and their defeat by the Romans in A.D. 70—which, by the way, is the reason the Sadducees are not mentioned in the Gospel of John. Their views were then passé.

How did the coming of Jesus impact our understanding of the afterlife?

Into this debate concerning new life and resurrection after death God sent Jesus, his one and only son, who reflected the very image and character of God (see for example Col. 1:15-20, Heb. 1:1-4, John 1:1-18). It was in the actual historical death of Jesus and in his miraculous resurrection and mysterious ascension into heaven that God provided humans with a divine demonstration of the supra time-space transcendent nature of the hope that characterizes the Christian understanding of eternity and heaven.

This Christian conception of resurrection from the dead, as Oscar Cullmann has so forcefully explained,[4] is very different from the Greek idea of immortality of the soul that continues today to be a popular philosophic construct for the afterlife—even among many Christians. Unfortunately, Christians—who have difficulty conceiving of God functioning in the realm of a supra time-space—often accept this popular misconception that relies on the idea of immortality of the soul because they have trouble understanding the biblical concept of bodily resurrection.

But immortality is a quality of God. Humans do not possess immortality on this earth. We are not immortal! We die. Death is real. But God can give humans immortality—in the Resurrection! The early Christians took their death and the death of Jesus very seriously. Death for them was an enemy—the final resource Satan had to bewitch and threaten believers into submitting to devilish patterns of life (1 Cor. 15:26, 54-57).

But in the resurrection of Jesus, God effectively displayed the means for Christians to conquer the grip of their "last enemy"—death—and that is the reason why Christians took Resurrection so seriously. The Resurrection provided them with the convincing answer to their mortality. They knew they were not worthy of God's grace or the promise of new life. Yet in the resurrection, God gave them victory over their greatest fears. Accordingly, Paul unapologetically announced that if there was no resurrection and if Christ had not been raised, then Christians would be fools and his preaching would be empty or meaningless (*kenos*; 1 Cor. 15:12-19). There is no doubt that Paul believed the resurrection of Jesus to be nothing less than the hinge point of Christianity. There would be no Christianity without the reality of the Resurrection.[5] That is the reason Christians have proclaimed: "Χριστὸς ἀνέστη! (*Christos aneste*) Yes, Christ is risen, indeed!"

What is the difference between immortality of the soul and the biblical view of the resurrection of the dead?

Why then do many Christians continue to hold on to the idea of immortality of the "soul" and play loose with the crucial significance of the resurrection of the dead? The answer lies in humanity's concern for understanding and controlling our destiny. We are not in control of this life or of the afterlife. We as Christians are still mortals.

While it is difficult for us as mere mortals to perceive the implications of God actually existing outside of the boundaries of time and space, it is even more difficult for us to conceive of the possibility that when people die, they actually exit time. Time and space provide the basic framework for almost all of human perception. But God is not a human, and God is not bound by time or space. Thus, when Jesus—God's Son, who became human for a brief period of time—announced that "before Abraham was, I am," he stunned his Jewish critics (John 8:58). His critics were stuck in time. Jesus was not! When Jesus became flesh, he entered not only his created world but also time—which he also created (John 1:2, 14).

Do you now see the problem for humanity in dealing with death? People who continue to live on in this world after they have buried their loved ones have great difficulty conceiving of what is happening to those loved ones while they themselves are still part of the creation's ongoing time-space sequence. The natural inclination then is to try and fix their lack of understanding concerning their loved ones' relationships to time and space. The easiest way to do so is by imagining that part of their loved one is immortal and does not die—namely, adopting the Greek view of "the soul." But Christians do not have to succumb to the unbiblical views of the Greeks. We need to let our loved ones die, into the hands of God who is both inside and outside of time and space!

That is what Paul was trying to do when he wrote 1 Thessalonians. The Christians in the Macedonian capital were seeing their friends die, and they were worried and became anxious about the gospel promises—especially in relation to time. Would they or those who had died miss the trumpet call of the Resurrection? Paul assured them: Don't worry; God is in charge! Well, would they know the time and who would get to heaven first? Again: Don't worry. Everyone will recognize the trumpet blast and get there in the same event (1 Thess. 4:11-18). We might ask how that is possible. The answer is: Don't worry because God is not bound by our limitations of time and space.

So, as Paul tells us: Relax and encourage others in our great hope of the Resurrection (1 Thess. 4:18). Also, keep your minds open on the issue of the interrelationship of supra-time and supra-space with God. Then you will discover, as Paul did, that to be absent from the body (our earthly tent—to die) is to be present (at home) with the Lord (2 Cor. 5:6-10). So, again I say: If you believe in Christ, then don't worry about issues of time and space. The Creator knows how to handle both of them.

What are the implications of the picture of heaven that emerge in the Book of Revelation?

In concluding these thoughts about death and eternity, I must not omit the Christian view of heaven, which for many is often encumbered with our understanding of place and space. How could a Christian writer like the seer of Revelation explain heaven? For him to do so, he had to use the space categories that were familiar to him and his readers. But in the attempt to achieve his goal, he actually had to explode those categories so they would stretch human thinking beyond earthly realities. The result is the magnificent description of heaven in Revelation 21 and 22. As I explained in my commentary on Revelation,[6] I would ask you to use your imagination as we review the seer's picture of heaven and to not be troubled by human logic or human definitions of items. But try to imagine the implied significance of those descriptors.

John defines heaven as "where" God dwells and where there is no more sorrow, pain, or death (21:3-4) and where all evil has been eliminated (21:8). Heaven is assumed to be up and the abode of evil down; therefore, heaven is linked to mountains and the Holy City of God will be brought down to the new earth (21:10). This city will be radiating as a precious jewel, and will have walls and gates to protect the people. (If John had lived longer, he probably would have described the heavenly city without walls. The Roman city of Beth Shean in Israel had no walls.) You would expect the walls to have gates—twelve of them representing the traditional idea of the people of God. Yet the foundations for these gates are built not on the traditional children of Israel but on the new people of God represented by the mission of Christ in the twelve apostles (21:11-14).

Although the seer knows that most ancient cities are viewed in two dimensions, he imagines this heavenly city in three dimensions—as an immense perfect cube—with plenty of room for all to enter. And naturally, all its dimensions are described in terms of the numbers twelve and a thousand (the huge number). Moreover, since the city is viewed as a precious place, it is pictured in terms of gold. But unlike earthly gold because it is absolutely clear, even the streets on which one walk are made of such a divinely inspired transparent material. The foundations of the walls are adorned with jewels, and each of the gates is made from a single pearl (21:15-21). (Imagination is a wonderful gift and can carry us to the clouds, but I have often asked what my students think was the size of the oysters that produced such magnificent jewels!) John has given us a wonderful vision of heaven.

Then he continues his fascinating picture by adding that there is no need for a temple nor for the sun and moon (light) in this divine city because God, the Almighty, and the Lamb are present and there will never be night nor evil in this setting (Rev. 21:22-27; cf. John 13:30 where night is also the symbol of evil). John concludes this glowing glimpse into heaven in Revelation 22 with a grand scene adapted from Ezekiel 42 of the refreshing river of life that flows from the joint throne of God and of the Lamb. This water of life is for those living on the edge of the desert the basic symbol of life (Rev. 21:6, 22:1; cf. John 7:37-38). Moreover, on both sides of this sustaining river John sees the historic tree of life (cf. Gen. 2:9, 3:22), which is one of the great uniting pictures of Revelation because it implies that there is no "wrong side of the tracks" in heaven! There is little I can add to such an encompassing description except to summon you to be alert and be prepared for the *parousia* (the presence or return of Christ) when time shall cease and the Lord will make all things new.

But in the meantime this message of the Book of Revelation has been sent so that Christians will live boldly confident in this world—not succumbing to the chaotic ways of the evil dragon (Revelation 12) or his political minions who do his bidding (Revelation 13) and who are represented by the beast of the sea (Rome, the nation that at that time controlled the world) and the evil, pseudo-lamb (the emperor Domitian, who for John embodied all the evil ways of Nero). Instead, Christians in the worldwide church (note the number seven in Rev. 1:11) are both warned and encouraged to live in integrity because Christ (see the description of the risen and ascended Jesus in Rev. 1:12-20) is with them and directing their faith communities (Revelation 2 and 3) to live according to their model, Jesus Christ. He has promised to seal them and sustain them (7:4, 14:1) and call them to endurance during their difficult times (cf. 13:9-10). Then ultimately, he will bring them to himself so that they may experience their great hope of his eternal presence (7:9-17, 11:15-17, 14:1-5, 20:4-6, 21:1–22:1-5).

Therefore, entrust your lives and service to Christ Jesus, my sons and friends, as you imitate his model of both lovingly relying on God and lovingly caring for others (Matt. 22:32-40). You will not go wrong if you follow that model because love is from God and everyone who makes love his/her way of life is born of God (1 John 1:7). Moreover, be sure to follow the leading of the Holy Spirit who through Christ is your companion and who will guide you into all truth (John 16:13). Place your hope in Almighty God, the beginning and the end, the only one powerful enough to bring you to your eternal destiny (Rev. 1:8). God bless all of you.

In Christ,
Dad / Dr. B.

Questions for Reflection

• What were your reactions to Dr. B.'s story of the woman's hair and the nature of corpses who have been buried for some time? Does it trouble you to think about the disintegration of your parents' bodies? Of your body? How do you integrate the idea of corpses with the creative ability of God? Does God need a body to assure the resurrection? Do you think Christians need to bury the full body? What do you think about cremation?

• What are your reactions to the suggestion of rethinking your views concerning space and time as they relate to death and the Resurrection? Had you imagined that God might be both inside and outside of time prior to reading this letter?

• What is your view concerning the discussion of ancient burial practices and ancient tombs?

• Have you been thinking about your life and death in terms of the immortality of the soul rather than the resurrection of the body? How do you react to the idea that immortality of the soul is a Greek concept and not a Christian idea?

• Is your idea of eternity tied to a concept of extended time? Why or why not?

• How do you picture heaven? Can you imagine how John might describe it if he was living in the twenty-first century? How might it be different than the way he described it in the first century? Do you not think that would be a fascinating experience to try?

Notes

[1] See my detailed discussion in "Excursus 33: Questions of Eternity: Where Is the Place? What Is It Like? How Do We Get There?" in Gerald L. Borchert, *John 12–21* in vol. 23B, *The New American Commentary* (Nashville: Broadman and Holman, 2002), 360-67.

[2] See Plato, *Phaedras*, 246-54.

[3] For an excellent sociological and theological analysis of the difference between the Pharisees and the Sadducees, see Louis Finkelstein, *The Pharisees: The Sociological Background of Their Faith* (Philadelphia: The Jewish Publication Society of America, 1962).

[4] See Oscar Cullmann, *Immortality of the Soul or Resurrection of the Dead: The Witness of the New Testament* (London: Epworth, 1958).

[5] See my discussion in Gerald L. Borchert, "The Resurrection," in *Review and Expositor*, 80.3 (Summer 1983), 401-15.

[6] Gerald L. Borchert, "The Book of Revelation" in *NLT Study Bible*, 2nd ed. (Carol Stream, IL: Tyndale House, 2008), 2162-63.

Chapter 14

Christian Worship

Dear Mark, Tim, and Friends:

After having read and approved more than a couple hundred doctoral theses on various topics related to worship and having taught worship to many additional students in a number of different programs, I have some deep concerns regarding worship. My concerns focus particularly on our current society that is marked by an intense narcissism—probably best captured, as my late colleague Robert Webber used to say, by the idea: "It's all about me!" You may ask why I would place a chapter on worship at the culminating point of a book about theology, ethics, and life. It is because I believe that a Christian's authentic life is the result of correct worship.

My comments here on worship are not focused on any particular Christian fellowship, as I have taught students from many denominations.[1] Neither is my concern primarily about the construction of worship services. (For guidance to such information, I suggest consulting the work of my former student and colleague Constance Cherry.[2]) Neither is my interest in this response about what we experience in a service of worship and over which we often stand in judgment. Worship is not about what is being done to us or for us, and it is surely not about our likes and dislikes or about our feelings.

What is Christian worship?
To put it bluntly, Christian worship is:
- not about a religious exercise (although it may involve religious practices);
- not primarily about music or prayer (although it may involve both);
- not about deciding for traditional, blended, or convergent worship services;
- not about buildings (I have worshipped around the world in all sorts of structures including mud huts, open fields, stadia, and town squares);
- not about using orchestras, talking drums, bands, or an organ;
- not about specific times such as 11:00 a.m. on Sundays or 6:00 p.m. on Saturdays;
- not about wearing a robe, a suit and tie, a dress, or a sweatshirt and blue jeans;

- not about using candles and/or incense;
- not about using a "handbook on worship" from a particular denomination;
- not about using wafers, leavened or unleavened bread, or hard crackers and wine, grape juice, or a substitute at a communion or eucharistic service;
- not about dunking, pouring, or sprinkling in baptism; and
- not just for Sundays or special church festivals throughout the year.

We like to argue about these matters and I suppose we will continue to do so like the rabbis in Jesus' day, but such arguments do not bring us closer to understanding genuine worship. While these issues may be of concern, Jesus warns in Matthew 23:23 about "religious nit-picking" and neglecting true evidences of authenticity in life and worship.

Before I continue, I want to remind you what I stated in my book, *Worship in the New Testament*: Worship involves "all of life."[3] This perspective is foundational to what the apostle Paul asserts in Romans 12:1-2 when he insists that Christians should turn over their "bodies to God" as "a living and holy sacrifice" (NLT). Dead or inanimate and impure sacrifices are not what God seeks. God wants sacrificial human beings, who have been declared "holy." When God receives these living offerings, God can and will do wonders with them.

Sacrificial, holy living is the key to worship. Nothing less is adequate, but we must always be aware that we cannot attain holy living on our own. We need the gracious work of God in our lives if we are to represent the holy God adequately. Such a concept is what Martin Luther in his own struggle finally discovered when he designated the authentic way of life as both *gabe und aufgabe* (gift and requirement). To be true worshippers, we must give ourselves to God. But we cannot do so without the gracious divine assistance of God's Spirit in our lives. Such a perspective is also the reason why I consider Robert Webber's little book, *Worship Is a Verb*, to be one of his most significant contributions.[4] Worship is an act of living with and for the living and holy God.

Accordingly, worship is about God and it involves us as mortals coming before the Almighty, who created us and accepted us through Jesus Christ in all our unworthiness. That word, "unworthiness," is crucial since it is not we but God's Son who is truly "worthy" because he died for our acceptance. Indeed, the very term worship is derived from the Anglo-Saxon term, *weorth-scipe*, which evolved into "worthship" and finally "worship." Worshiping God means ascribing "supreme worth" to the Lord.

In the Book of Revelation, John tries to sum up the amazing significance of Jesus' coming when he proclaims Jesus to be the "Lamb of God" and the one who is "worthy" to receive "power, and wealth, and wisdom, and might, and honor, and glory and blessing" (John 1:29, 36; Rev. 5:5-6, 12). In this magnificent sevenfold ascription to Jesus, one has the feeling of "Wow!" and of understanding why the elders of Revelation—who represent the biblical understanding of the people of God/the church—fall in worship before this Lamb and before God who sits enthroned before all creation (5:14).

Why do we speak of Christian worship as Trinitarian?

Christ's self-giving death, powerful resurrection, and glorious exaltation for us (Heb. 1:3) and his joining the Father in sending the Holy Spirit to be our constant Advocate (Paraclete, John 15:26) is the reason we Christians worship the Triune God.

The concept of Jesus in the Trinity is for most people a bewildering idea and is not easy to define because the Triune God does not fit the parameters of human logic. For the early disciples, the relationship of Jesus to God was foggy though fairly easy to understand when it came to Jesus calling God his Father, but it was more difficult for them to perceive when Jesus said he was "the way to the Father." Then, it became much harder when he added that "he who has seen me has seen the Father." And it probably blew their minds when he said, "I am in the Father and the Father in me" (John 14:6-11). The categories of God's time and space do not compute in our human minds, and that is the reason why our explanations and the examples we use concerning God and the divine reality fail miserably.

We can, of course, deny that such a reality as God exists, but such a conclusion leaves us with scores of unanswered questions. The alternative is that we will have to live with our feeble attempts and approximations at understanding God and the Trinity.

But I would further warn all of us that after trying to explain God or making our clever constructs concerning divine attributes and actions, we should not then attempt to use those constructs to suggest or posit that we actually understand what we have said. One example of such unhelpfulness is the church's historic arguments over the *filioque* clause ("and the Son") concerning the Trinity in the church's post-Nicene confession(s) as revised and expanded at Constantinople and later. The theology of the Trinity is difficult for the clergy to explain and is particularly opaque for many of the laity when it comes to understanding the Holy Spirit in relation to the so-called sending and/or proceeding from God. In his gospel, John indicates that both the Father (John 14:26) and the Son (15:26) are responsible for the sending of the Spirit. The Eastern (Orthodox) and Western (Roman Catholic) wings of the church, however, have had bitter arguments over whether the Spirit proceeded from the Father or from both the Father and the Son,[5] as Augustine argued so intensely.

Why is mystery inherent in our understanding of worship?

Our repeated attempts to construct statements of faith that can be confessed by the church in a "worship activity" actually can result in frustration of understanding because we desperately try to explain the impossible in search of an intelligent conclusion to mystery. But we must be very careful with our assumptions of knowledge concerning the divine. Although the post-apostolic fathers of the church went to great lengths to revise their articulated definitions and formulas concerning the nature of the personae in the Trinity, it behooves us not to assume that those definitions actually explain mystery or are either final or inerrant. For example, it can frustrate our neat thinking concerning the order of the Trinity to see in 1 Peter 1:2 and Revelation 1:4-5 that both have the Spirit listed second when we usually consider that the Spirit must appear third in our church's thinking and formulas.

To approach the subject in another way, do you remember those storm stories in the Gospel of Mark (4:35-41, 6:45-51)? In the first story, Jesus is asleep on a pillow in the stern of the boat when a typical fierce windstorm comes down through the Valley of the Pigeons (or Doves) on to the Sea of Galilee. The disciples are terrified. In panic they cry out to Jesus, who awakes and shouts to the storm "Shut up!" (Greek translation: "Be Muzzled!"). The storm stops. Then Jesus asks them why they were afraid and why they did not have faith.

The second storm story in Mark is slightly varied, but the disciples are again out on the Sea of Galilee at night when a storm comes up and Jesus calmly walks on the water as though he is taking a late evening stroll. Thinking he is a ghost, they scream in terror. He responds for them to be courageous and not to fear, and then identifies himself as "I am" and climbs into the boat. The storm immediately ceases.

Now both of these stories are the background to important reactions by the disciples. In the first story they respond with a sense of wonder and a question: "Who is this guy?" He is indeed "spooky" (4:41). In the second story the experience is again utterly shocking.

When people encounter Jesus, they meet mystery! But the mystery of Jesus, like that of God and the Holy Spirit, does not compute in our human minds. The mystery of God baffles us: we can neither fully understand such mystery, nor can we control it. In academia, we have constructed a wonderful expression for encountering God and divine mystery. We call it the *mysterium tremendum*. By this construct, I suppose we think we understand it. But I prefer to say that the Triune God is spooky! We may try to analyze our experiences with God, but in the end, mystery still remains mystery. And it is this mystery that is the focus of our worship.

The early Christians recognized that when Jesus came to this planet, he represented the full reality of God in human flesh. That is the reason why John included the historic confession of Thomas: "My Lord and my God!" (John 20:28). Nothing less than the identification of Jesus with *YHWH*, the mysterious God of the Old Testament, would suffice in his portrait of Jesus as God's incarnate messenger. That is the reason why Christians place Jesus together with the Father and the Spirit in the Trinity as the central focus of Christian worship.

What are some general implications of Christian worship?

We completely misunderstand Christian worship if we think and speak about it apart from the central configuration of the personae we call the Triune God. Focusing on our feelings and our likes and dislikes—as is done in our worship wars—rather than focusing on God renders many of our conversations about worship as misdirected and meaningless. The entire concept of worship is not about us. It is about honoring God for the marvelous acts of the creation and for the incredible redemption (saving/freeing) of humans from their sinfulness and lack of integrity.

Many people have also been misguided in thinking about worship as performing before other humans. Worship must be focused on God or it is not worship.

In addition, there is the issue of corporate worship. While individuals can worship separately, there is an amazing strength to be gained through worshiping with others. Jesus made it clear that "where two or three are gathered in my name, I am among them" (Matt. 18:20).

Worship involves various thought patterns and senses. For example, it encompasses left brain verbal thinking and reasoning such as preaching, witnessing, and rationalizing about God. It also draws on right brain symbolic experiences such as corporately participating in baptism and the Lord's Supper or Eucharist. Christian worship should involve the whole person or the entire self. Accordingly, worship leaders should promote the legitimacy of right brain experiences in worship, such as those of the:

- Eye—emphasizing color and form such as in art, drama, decoration, and the beauty of God's creation;
- Ear—participating in singing, hearing music and bell ringing, and hearing the sounds of birds, waterfalls, thunder, etc.;
- Nose—reflecting on the wonders of nature, the various smells that people associate the gifts and presence of God in cooking at fellowship meals, the anointing of the sick, and the debated issues of using incense and other sweet odors;
- Mouth—tasting foods at community meals and participating in Communion; and
- Touch—experiencing baptism, a hand on one's shoulder in prayer, remembering the grasping of Jesus' feet in Matt. 28:9 and the practice of foot washing initiated by Jesus in John 13.[7]

Excluding such right brain aspects of worship in the name of proper decorum or practice can minimize the full range of possibilities for worshipping God.

It is crucial to recognize that the two major actions/sacraments/ordinances of God's people in worship provide Christians with dramatic models or summary portraits of the way in which they should live the Christian life. Baptism, as Paul so vividly explains in Ephesians and Colossians, represents the pattern of transformation that takes place when the believer "puts off" the old way of life and consciously "puts on" the new way of Christ in moving through the three stages, beginning with faith and justification to love and the sanctification process to hope and our glorification. In a similar pattern, the Lord's Supper or Eucharist strategically depicts the three perspectives of the Christian who must:

- repeatedly glance back to "remember" the death and resurrection of Jesus as our divinely bestowed basis of forgiveness and new life;
- accept the awesome responsibility of depending upon Christ and currently living in him just as the elements are "given to us" for our present living; and

- trust in his provision for our future as we "proclaim" that he "will come again" to receive us to himself—even though we are hardly worthy of that hope.

How does Jesus help us gain perspective on worship for our lives?

By contrast to the way the Jewish religious leaders lived in a straightjacket of tradition and form, Jesus is portrayed in the Gospels as a person with a great sense of freedom.[8] He heals on the Sabbath (e.g. John 5:1-14), readily touches "unclean" lepers (e.g. Matt. 8:3), and critiques the enshrined traditions of the religious elite (e.g., "You have heard . . . but I say . . ." [see Matt. 5:21-48]). He defends his disciples when they pluck grain while walking through fields and after rubbing the kernels and blowing the husks, they eat the "harvested" food, thereby breaking a number of staunchly protected rabbinic rules regarding the Sabbath (e.g. Mark 2:23-28). So unencumbered by the rules of the establishment is Jesus, he dares to overturn the tables of the money changers in the very precincts of the Temple (Mark 11:15-18).

Yet the freedom of Jesus is uniquely balanced by his genuine sense of obedience to God, his Father (John 5:19-20, 30), and to his own strategic place in the fulfillment of the Scriptures (Mark 12:10-11). Indeed, Jesus is so aware of the intended implications of the scriptural texts that he asserts confidently that not a "jot or a dot" will be at variance with God's intentions in the biblical texts (Matt. 5:17-18). But while the rabbis are literalists and focused on words, Jesus is always focused on the intentionality of God in the Scriptures. This difference is crucial for Jesus and leads to his multiple conflicts with the religious leadership of his day, not merely over their precious Sabbath rules but also with the many other interpretations of the 613 debated rules of the rabbis (e.g. Mark 4:4-6; 7:1-8, 9-13; 10:2-9; 12:13-17, 18-27).[9]

To illustrate this face-off on worship between Jesus and the religious leaders more clearly, remember the decree in Exodus 31:14 that anyone who does "any work" on the Sabbath shall be "put to death" (or "be cut off from among his people"). This statement became the basis for the strict Sabbath observance patterns by the rabbis, and they supported their interpretations with the fact that even God observed a Sabbath rest in the creation story (Gen. 2:3). But even the rabbis soon realized that some exceptions were necessary in the face of impending perils or hazards such as war, especially after some pious Maccabean fighters were killed when they stopped fighting the pagan Syrians on the Sabbath!

Similarly, the rabbis made another exception in the case of circumcision. In understanding their legal logic, it is important to realize that the rabbis generally agreed that various laws were to be given different legal weight. Sabbath law was regarded as the primary liturgical law, but circumcision was given preference since it was a matter of Jewish identity.

Then Jesus comes onto the scene and questions the rabbis' neat compromise regarding the Sabbath and forcefully questions their priority of circumcision over healing (note John 7:23-24). For Jesus, something in their formulas has been badly misconstrued when the well-being of a person is rated lower than a person's ritual actions or identity. And if that is not enough to upset the rabbis' neat categories for dealing with the Sabbath, Jesus attacks their foundational understanding of Sabbath itself—that it has priority over humanity. He reminds them that humans were not made for Sabbath but the Sabbath was installed by God for human benefit (Mark 2:27). Then to top off the view of Jesus, he declares that he is in fact like God and is Lord over the Sabbath (Matt. 12:8)!

The obvious result of such an argument by Jesus is the demolition of the rabbinic "House of Cards." Do you understand why it was virtually impossible for the rabbis and Jesus to exist side by side in Palestine? One of them had to give or go! Jesus became the sacrificial lamb.

So, we must repeatedly ask: What would happen to our worship patterns if Jesus came again today? Just think about the fusses we have concerning worship patterns, church order, seating arrangements, church officers' roles, types of music used, preaching styles, meaning of sacraments or ordinances, accoutrements and symbols used, and so on.

Still, I want you to sense something more in the above illustration. Notice that in these segments of the gospel arguments—in Matthew, Mark, and John—Jesus is amazingly free to represent God's will for the Sabbath and at the same time is completely faithful in representing God's purposes for humanity in worship and in asserting the true meanings of scriptural texts.

What should these reflections suggest to us for our life and worship in the twenty-first century?

I propose that in leading people in worship, we need to recognize that it is not necessary to follow a pattern of worship practiced by our grandparents, by the early church, in the Reformation, or in the time when our denomination was founded. We can be innovative in style, in music, in drama, in structures, in the use of accoutrements such as banners and the like, and in meeting times but not in the primary focus of our worship! At a minimum, true worship should:

- focus on God and the fact that God is marvelous and mysterious—greater than our understanding.
- recognize that God is caring and loving—like a gentle parent who accepts us despite our sin and toying with chaos and in love wants to meet and "walk" with us.
- assist us in acknowledging our humanity and lead us to confess our unworthiness by coming in reverence before the forgiving God.
- lead us to offer our deep gratitude for our Lord's gift of new life and to respond by bringing our praise, honor, and thanksgiving to the Lord for the continuing marvelous grace shown to us through our Savior, Jesus.
- engender a sense of assurance to live in the power of the loving Christ; and
- commission us to communicate that love and the forgiveness of God to others.

In addition, our worship format and practice should be relevant and meaningful to the people who are worshipping—neither being so elevated and unworldly that it is meaningful only to a few specialists nor so mundane, chaotic, and careless that it is inconsequential and lacking in genuine respect for God.

But I would assert that our primary focus must be on the Triune God and not on any of us as humans. Worship should be done as well as possible but not for the purpose of gaining human praise. When the focus is placed on us as humans, it ceases to be worship and becomes performance. This distinction is crucial for helping people understand what the major focus of worship should be in our "me-centered generation." It is perhaps the hardest lesson for Christians to learn. Moreover, we who are worship leaders must be constantly sensitive to the subtle temptation that comes to us—namely, putting ourselves in the place of God.

If we fail to make God the center of worship, our churches and faith communities will collapse internally into groups engaged in arguments and self-centered conflicts. People will lose evangelistic fervor and mission outreach, and our in-fighting will lead to division and lack spiritual awareness. But when our focus is placed on the Triune God, we should begin to sense that our attitudes shift to that of genuine, humble, self-giving service for the Lord. Thus, to lead worship appropriately, we must have a sincere humility before God. All worship leaders of any Christian community should read and reread Philippians 2:1-16 on the importance of having the model of Christ's humility inscribed on their hearts. Then, together we can live authentically and sing: "To God be the glory!"

God bless you in your worship and service for the Lord. You will never fully wrap your minds around the Triune God, but if you seek to honor God, you can be confident that God will be present in your lives and will wrap the secure divine self around you!

Finally, remember that no matter how much spiritual insight you may receive during the course of your lives, keep vividly in mind this stern warning that John received in the final chapter of Revelation (22:9): "Worship only God!"

In Christ Jesus,
Dad / Dr. B.

Questions for Reflection

- Why do you think Dr. B. began his letter on worship with a long list of negatives?
- Why do you think Dr. B. criticized arguments over definitions? Why does he seem to like the word "spooky"?
- Why is Dr. B. so committed to saying that worship is not about us? Why is he critical of viewing worship as performance? Explain.
- Why do you think Jesus felt completely free to break the enshrined rules of the rabbis?
- Why do you think Dr. B. distinguishes between literalism and intentionality? Is that distinction important to you? Why or why not?
- Do you understand the concept of the "Triune God"? Explain. Is it important to you? Why? Or, why not?

Notes

[1]My students have come from a great variety of backgrounds: Church of God (instrumental and non- instrumental), Charismatic and Pentecostal groups, Mennonites and various Baptists, Lutherans of the Missouri Synod and other synods, Methodists and Presbyterians, and the so-called high churches such as Anglicans, Episcopalians, Roman Catholics, and Orthodox.

[2]Constance M. Cherry, *The Worship Architect: A Blueprint for Designing Culturally Relevant and Biblically Faithful Services* (Grand Rapids: Baker Academic, 2010).

[3]See Gerald L Borchert, *Worship in the New Testament: Divine Mystery and Human Response* (St. Louis: Chalice Press, 2008).

[4]See either Robert E. Webber, *Worship is a Verb: Eight Principles for Transforming Worship* (Peabody, MS: Hendrickson, 1992, 2000, etc.). or *Worship is a Verb: Celebrating God's Mighty Acts of Salvation* (1996).

[5]For the Nicene Creed, see Henry Bettenson, *Documents of the Christian Church* (London: Oxford University Press, 1956), 34-37.

[6]See the helpful discussion in J.N.D. Kelly, *Early Christian Doctrine*, rev. ed. (San Francisco: Harper & Row, 1960, 1978), 252-279, especially at 274-275.

[7]See my remarks under "Issues in Communicating the Gospel to a Biblically Illiterate Generation" in Gerald L. Borchert, *Portraits of Jesus for an Age of Biblical Illiteracy* (Macon, GA: Smyth & Helwys, 2016), 12-17.

[8]See Gerald L. Borchert, "The Lord of Form and Freedom: A New Testament Perspective on Worship," *Review and Expositor*, 80.1 (Winter 1983), 5-18.

[9]I would remind you that the Jewish Mishnah is a record of the debates over what the rabbis considered to be the most important rules. See Herbert Danby, *The Mishnah: Translated from the Hebrew with Introduction and Brief Explanatory Notes* (London: Oxford University Press, 1933).

Questions Related to the Future

Dear Mark, Tim, and Friends:

As we arrive at this final segment of my letters and questions to you, I want to touch briefly on a number of very difficult issues that are already in focus or will soon be coming before us. I also want you to realize that we are in a sense coming full circle from the creation and temptation stories of humanity in chapter 1 where we discussed chaos (Genesis 1–3). In the biblical story the cunning serpent tricks humans into thinking they can become "Godlike" in their knowledge (3:5), when in fact humans already have the potential of acting either against or with God.

In this section, while I do not intend to treat the issues in detail, I want us to recognize that the ways in which we deal with all the issues before us actually illustrate for us how much or how little we presume to be like God in our various circumstances—indeed, how much we act like or contrary to the ways of God. Thus, I think these questions can provide us with some helpful insights for measuring how "Godlike" or "Christlike" we actually are.

As we Christians struggle with the issues discussed here and throughout this work, we should bear in mind that perhaps there are some very unsettling questions already present and even more on the horizon that are looming large as we look to the future. These questions will involve the necessity of coming to grips with the realities of life itself. Likewise, we are and will be confronted by the actual limits within the nature of space, time, and resources for life that are available to humans within our world. We are and will continue to be impacted by the human unquenchable desire for "more"—the human lust for privilege, power, and wealth, namely its self-centeredness and greed.

Some of these realities have in the past led to serious conflicts and intense warfare among humans. Unfortunately, I can foresee that some of these matters will continue to enhance chaos among people and will likely also unhinge even governments. Christians will be forced to wrestle with some deep questions about life and about unwanted crises within their contexts. And followers of Christ will have to make some difficult decisions in the near future. Thus, while there are many issues waiting to be addressed, let me briefly highlight just a few.

Drugs

Coming generations will continue to face the issue of drug use in many forms. Inherent within this issue are at least three major questions pertaining to the great desire among humans for using chemical means to achieve an escape from pain, anxiety, and trouble and to achieve a pseudo-fairytale-like feeling of utopia; the toying with recreational limits; and the insatiable desire of people to profit from the woes and desires of others.

I turn first to the issue of greed. Since the world is now more interconnected than in past eras, people (perhaps in deep poverty) in distant lands can grow or manufacture (often in secluded locations) vast quantities of stimulants and narcotics at relatively low costs. Then entrepreneurs can market through secret and illegal connections those products to people who have been "hooked" on them—often thousands of miles away. In the process, little care is given by distributors to the fate of those who are the pathetic recipients of those products. Profit is all that matters—even if those products may be contaminated with deadly substances such as arsenic. No guarantees are made: the products are already illegal and have been obtained and transported through undercover means.

Illegal drugs are not the only aspect of the problem, however. Legitimate pharmaceutical tobacco and beverage companies have even baited medical doctors with financial and other incentives to prescribe rather freely opiates to patients, with the result that those patients become dependent upon such medications as they seek to cope with painful living or long-term depression. Greed is clearly not absent from the medical profession, although I would hasten to state that most persons I know in the medical field are very caring and are clearly concerned for their patients. That may not be so true of those who are engaged in producing the materials for the current rage of "vaping" or of the growing use of marijuana.

An additional problem with pharmaceutical companies involves new combinations of drugs and their processing. For example, a physician friend responded to my question of why a generic drug that had been available from the non-restricted list was suddenly placed on the dangerous and restricted list. After inquiry he told me that the company marketing the new combined medication, which sold for an exorbitant price, had pressured the state to place the old drug on the restricted list so that the new drug combination would not be disadvantaged. Greed is definitely a quality of the darkened nature of humanity (Eph. 4:19).

A major issue that is emerging involves the growing use of recreational drugs such as marijuana/cannabis. With the legalization of its use in a number of states, people may be hamstrung in the future with problems at least comparable to the use of tobacco and alcohol. In this respect I am reminded of an interesting experience that took place when I was the president of a downtown Kiwanis Club in a previous city where we lived. The city leaders were concerned about the growing drug problem among students in the school system and asked a respected Christian physician, who was the chief of staff at one of the hospitals, and me to form a drug education committee. The doctor became the chair of the committee, and I was appointed the chair of the drug education speakers' committee for the city.

One intriguing part of that role was the placing of at least one medical doctor and one lawyer on each of the speaking teams. It was priceless to see how those professionals who often distrusted each other because of legal cases were able to work together on the common task of helping to prevent young people and children from falling into the misuse of drugs. Yet, in sharing their experiences with the rest of the speakers, I remember vividly how one team came back from an engagement and told the group how they were stunned by several students from one high school who challenged their mission by asking them: "Do the team members use alcohol?" When the team begrudgingly admitted that they did, then the students asked them: "Why should we listen to the team because we know that alcohol is also a drug?" That experience unlocked a key issue for most of the members in the group, and they began to ask themselves: "What is the moral difference between the recreational use of alcohol and the recreational use of marijuana and other drugs?" And I would now add: Why should young people listen to elders who smoke and who warn them about the medical dangers of vaping?

Such experiences have forced me to recognize how difficult it is to deal with moral issues in a so-called free society even if there are medical hazards associated with those issues. Young people are very aware of the way adults operate, and they are not fooled by their double standards. Moreover, they assume they are above endangerment. Unfortunately, I have had to watch them learn that they are not invulnerable. (And that conclusion applies to all humans.)

In addressing groups, I often remind people that Paul in Romans 1:16-32 sets out in bold statements the plight of humanity that refuses to honor God. Humans go through a rather clear pattern of moral decline in which God gives them over to the dissolution of their hearts (or wills), the dishonoring of their bodily passions (or physical desires), and the degeneration of their minds (or thought processes) so that they not only engage in ill-conceived practices but also seek others to join them and thus attempt to justify their sinful actions—which is the basis for all sorts of conspiracies (see vv. 24, 26, 28, 32). I suggest that you ponder this statement of Paul so as to understand more clearly the decadent state of humanity. Give special attention to this pattern of human decline while you consider the remaining sections of this chapter, because many now posit a future for this world without God.

Refugees and Movements of People

We who live in Canada and the United States of America know that most of our historical families did not come from North America. The migration particularly of Europeans from their homelands to seek a better life in the Americas has been one example in which the nationals or natives became expendable when the people from so-called "Christian" nations took over territories that were once the homes of what had been mistakenly called the "Indians" by our ancestors. Today, humans in other nations find that their homelands are being demanded by ruthless forces or by natural disasters that are preventing them from surviving adequately. As a result, we see many people seeking to find refuge elsewhere in lands already occupied. This current movement of people is causing great trauma in the world, particularly in the more prosperous nations that are feeling the pangs of chaos from the new arrivals.

I would remind you that when our faith ancestors such as Abraham moved from southern Mesopotamia (now modern Iraq) to Haran and then into the narrow land bridge of Palestine and westward into Egypt, they were probably part of a people movement. And when Moses led the people out of Egypt, scholars speculate that this event could also have been part of a people movement when the Shepherd Pharaohs (the fifteenth dynasty of Hyksos rulers from Palestine) were displaced in Egyptian history.

Today, Middle Easterners are swarming into Europe, and Central Americans and others are swarming into North America in search of a better life. Moreover, Africa is also in major turmoil. People movements are present in major numbers, and they are traumatizing both the arriving and the settled people in the land. In this current situation, there are many questions that face Christians in the more prosperous receiving nations. Even when they are not stated openly, the questions are: "Why can't we make people stay where they belong and not trouble us?" Or, "Why don't we enforce civility among those other rulers?" These questions apply also to the movements in Africa and elsewhere.

Our questions, of course, raise other questions related to civility (even in our own countries) on how we judge the lack of civility and who is competent and righteous enough to do the judging. The dream, of course, was that after World War II, the United Nations would be able to defuse such problems. While the U.N. has acted in some very helpful ways, changing the minds and hearts of humanity and enforcing civility is not in its purview or power. So, we are left with many questions:

- While we can do battle and force some tyrants out of power, what does it actually mean to force tyrants out of office in a world where evil and chaos are clearly present—even in the prosperous nations?
- Nations have gone to war for many reasons, but have they attained civility as the result?
- What really was accomplished when the West went to war with ISIS?
- To what extent can war assure us of civility among nations?

On the other hand, the questions can be reversed.
- How should refugees from such so-called demeaning nations be treated when they appear at the boarders of European and North American nations?
- Do Christians want refugee people in their neighborhoods?
- How should Christians react if these refugee people take jobs and cause the prosperous nations to suffer a lower standard of living by their presence?

These questions are indeed taxing, and most of the time we do not even attempt to answer them because they stretch our integrity to the point of implosion.

Yet do we not think that Jesus might have a perspective on these matters? Or do we not even want to add Jesus and his views about the poor, the hungry, and the dispossessed into our thinking about such people?

I will close this section with a message I received from some missionaries to Greece who stood recently with Albanian friends at their induction ceremony as they recited their vows for American citizenship:

> . . . many people, here and in Greece, are tempted to view immigrants as either hobos or hippies, unwilling to keep legitimate citizenship promises. I have not found this pre-judgment to be valid. My faith teaches me that immigrants are human beings, made in God's image and beloved ones for whom Christ died; thus, they are worthy of respect and appreciation in themselves. And I have found them to be trustworthy and dependable friends on whom I have often counted. I have rarely been disappointed in my immigrant friends—actually far less often than among my fellow citizens.

I suspect that this issue will not go away and it will measure us in our "Godlikeness" and Christian integrity! And that brings up another issue:

Riches and Wealth

In so-called Western Christianity we have neatly painted the concern about riches in very faint pastel colors. Do you not think that the messages of Jesus must have been bold and shocking—even to the disciples? My introducing this subject immediately after the discussion on refugees will probably raise all sorts of red flags. Nevertheless, I ask: How do you react to the story of the rich man, when Jesus says that the man lacks just one thing and that he should sell all he has and give it to the poor, then (and probably only then) come and follow him (Luke 18:22)? And, oh yes, the Gospels do say that it stuns the disciples (cf. Mark 10:24), Indeed, a small but forceful conclusion is added to the story by Mark indicating that Jesus also says "it is easier for a camel to go through the eye of a needle than for a rich man to enter the kingdom of God" (10:25).

I wonder why some interpreters have suggested that Jesus did not really mean that it is virtually impossible for a person who is rich to enter God's kingdom. Why have some tried to identify the "eye of a needle" with a low-entrance gate to an ancient city? That argument will just not work; it is a later construct. Jesus wanted his disciples to understand that wealth can have a serious negative effect on the possibility of discipleship and acceptance by God. In today's Western world where many of us are wealthy by comparison to the rest of the planet and the incredible wealth of a few is mushrooming at an alarming rate, are we taking this warning about riches seriously? It may be worth consulting our measuring tape on "Godlikeness" in this issue of riches.

Jesus did not leave the disciples in total confusion over this statement: he reminded them that human determination is not the answer to God's acceptance (10:27). Yet the way one responds to wealth and possessions is a key factor in recognizing who or what is primary or revered in one's life. Money is important to functioning in life, and the way one treats money is a major clue to what or who is "God" for that person. With wealth a person can do much good in the world, or it can become an idol in one's life. Indeed, it can be the "root of evil" for a person (1 Tim. 6:10). In the Lucan parable of the rich farmer who decides to build bigger barns, store up his possessions, and retire in ease, Jesus calls him a "fool" because he is not "rich toward God." And Jesus adds that the man's life will be taken from him that very night (Luke 12:19-21).

If we claim to be Christians, where do our money and possessions fit into that claim? Where do those who have desperate needs fit into the use of our money and possessions? These are tough questions. Mere words will not answer them. They will be answered by our lives!

War

The potential for war always seems to be in the background of much of humanity's history, including modern times. We may offer propositions for ending war, but if one nation seeks to intimidate or gain an advantage over another nation, it does not take long for there to emerge discussions on the possibility of armed conflict. Moreover, justifications for such potential reactions are easily forthcoming. Preventing armed conflict has been a dream of some politicians who realize that the cost of human life and resources is astronomical. Such was the vision of both the League of Nations and the United Nations, which have had a modicum of success—when the major power brokers among nations have wanted to cooperate! But when one or two major powers have been unwilling to agree to cooperation and see opportunities for advancement, then war is usually the result.

What are Christians to do in such circumstances? Debates focusing on "just war" and "pacifism" theories were especially prominent among proponents during and after World War II. While I do not wish to re-engage those debates here, I would ask you: "Is there any point in playing the blame game in war?" Does it really help? I know there are villains in war just as there are villains today who might be willing to punch a red button that fires intercontinental ballistic missiles into space. But is it possible that the reasons for tension are not merely one-sided? Power struggles are difficult to analyze—economically and otherwise. Are there not multiple reasons for engaging in war? Can you think of some?

But this issue of war brings up another concern. Where do you think God is in the issue of war? Is God on the side of America?

This issue was forcefully brought home to me when I served as the research assistant to Dr. Otto Piper at Princeton University. Because of his writings on ethics, the Gestapo in Nazi Germany gave him twenty-four hours to leave the country. As a result, during the Second World War he had one son in the German military and one son in the American forces. As we talked, he said to me: "Jerry, I know a little of how God feels in war." His son in Germany was killed.

Princeton had a tradition of reading in chapel the names and places of combat for graduates and close relatives of staff members who were killed in battle. Dr. Piper's son's name was treated accordingly. Some students were very displeased that a German's name was read out in the chapel.

How would you feel about such a practice if it was your son? How do you react to the question: Is God for you, an American?

Perhaps if we started turning away from justifying our engagements in war and started to think more like God, we might be able to consider better solutions for entering into wars in the first place. Do you think you could be a peacemaker for Christ? I think Jesus said that they would be called the children of God (Matt. 5:9).

The Termination of Life, Euthanasia, and Dying with Dignity

Having mentioned the issues of death and war, I turn now to the foundational Christian view of humanity, which is rooted in the reverence and sanctity of life as a gift of God. On the basis of such a presupposition, Scripture views death as humanity's "last enemy" (1 Cor. 15:26) that will be banished or thrown into the lake of fire after the devil is destroyed (Rev. 20:14). In the Bible, life is viewed as extremely important and taking the life of another person has historically been understood as a very sinful, evil act (Gen. 4:7-16) that should be punished by God or the state. This is the basis for the biblical view of *lex talionis* ("eye for eye," Exod. 21:23, Lev 24:19).

The Old Testament gives little attention to the afterlife, with the focus instead on the present life and the goal of living as long as possible and having many children and grandchildren—particularly sons and grandsons to complete one's genealogy. The thought of an early death is viewed as a divine curse (cf. Hezekiah's prayer in 2 Kgs. 20:1-11). So, the stories of Saul and his servant falling on their swords and Ahithophel hanging himself following their failures represent two unusual instances of suicide in the Hebrew Bible (1 Sam. 31:4-5, 2 Sam. 17:23).

In our court system, attempted self-termination of life (attempted suicide) has been treated as a felony and is usually punishable. Of course, there is little that can be done to punish the person in the case of actual suicide, but some insurance policies include a clause vitiating the policy for suicide in the initial years of activation.

The issue of arranged early termination to life (*euthanasia*: Greek for a "good/easy death"), however, is being thrust upon the American society by recent pressure and decisions in some states. Recognizing, permitting, or allowing as a legitimate legal decision the death of a person who desires to "die with dignity" has generally been based upon or rooted in intense suffering, pain, or trauma. The assumed understanding is that such a person would likely die shortly anyway, so it is argued that releasing a person from suffering is a justifiable act.

But there is a great debate on the assisted application of this process that usually involves the lethal intravenous injection of a drug such as pentothal. The debate usually centers on some controversial technical distinctions of the law and in medical practice regarding the point at which one moves from "killing" to "allowing (or perhaps assisting) a person to die peacefully." For many people, the distinction falls between active and passive voluntary euthanasia. But there are those who assert the legitimacy of the former as well as the latter. Nevertheless, we are approaching the place where doctors and lawyers are wrestling with issues that were once left to God or chance. The basic reason is that medical science has evolved to the point where it is possible to make such distinctions, especially with those who are in a vegetative state or who are in intense suffering that can be relieved but that does not lead to healing. The call for the legalization of certain types of euthanasia in many states is probably only a matter of time, and some states are already viewing those patterns with increasing interest.

The issue is further intensified when we focus on the question of a person's free will. Already we permit the legitimacy of living wills that allow persons to state prior to becoming unconscious that medical intervention should not take place in a situation that would require extraordinary measures to keep them alive. Questions then arise:

- Is adherence to living wills as far as we will go in legitimizing the termination of life?
- Will we move beyond the wishes stated in living wills to acceptance of active voluntary euthanasia?
- Under what circumstances will voluntary euthanasia be allowed?
- Will voluntary euthanasia be allowed for helplessness, extreme depression, or other causes?
- Will doctors be required, or merely allowed, to follow the wishes of a person?
- Could medical people be charged if they refuse to accept a person's wishes or will?
- How important is the will of the person who wishes to die?

These questions are hovering in the future, and Christians will have to consider these matters very seriously.

Abortion

Abortion is the induced or voluntary termination of a pregnancy that extinguishes and removes a fetus that—depending on one's definition—has been "alive" in a mother's womb. (Involuntary abortions are often referred to as "miscarriages" and are not the focus of this present discussion.)

Most discussions in Christian circles on this issue begin with references to the reverence and the sanctity of life. For me and countless other Christians, there is no question that life is precious. Taking life, therefore, has been generally regarded as a violation of God's will for humanity and the usual response has been based to a greater or lesser degree on the pattern of *lex talionis*—"eye for eye." But what shall we say about the question of abortion? If a woman desires an abortion and follows through on that desire, should we demand her life for the life of the fetus? Unfortunately, that issue is not quite as clear in the Bible as many have assumed, so we must not jump to conclusions.

Almost nothing is stated in the Old Testament concerning abortion. But the one text that is present is usually conveniently avoided in the condemnations of abortion. That text seems to run counter to the idea that a fetus is regarded as a "living being." Exodus 21:22 states that if two men are in a physical struggle and happen to engage a woman who is pregnant so that she suffers the loss of the fetus, but no other harm occurs, the one who hurt her must pay a fine. That text does not seem to imply that the fetus is yet recognized as a sustaining and living being—only one that is potentially a living being. We may ask: Why did the Bible not give us more direction on this matter? The answer probably is that the ancients did not expect people would consider abortions. Therefore, most theologians who write on this subject avoid beginning with this biblical text but start with what they consider is a general understanding of God's will for humans.

Is this pattern legitimate in the case of abortion? Perhaps, but not totally! It is possible to arrive at a completely unbiblical and an unethical perspective by providing a partial answer. For example, if a woman is raped and becomes pregnant and if the law refuses to allow for an abortion, then the woman must carry an unwanted child or be punished. But if she does not want such a child, is it possible that such a view is unjust? Yet such a view is the perspective of some advocates of strict anti-abortion! Some proponents have even claimed that women who have abortions are "murderers." Indeed, recently a woman in the Carolinas—who was engaged in a struggle and was shot so that the baby was aborted—was temporarily charged with a felony for not fleeing the scene to save the fetus, whereas the one who shot her was exonerated. Such is the confused current condition of the law and its enforcement in some states. Strong so-called "righteous" feelings can preempt logic and equity.

So, how are Christians to react in such cases? Jesus was not tied to rules, but he was concerned with the intentions of God for rules. And as is evident, the Old Testament text of Exodus 21:22 was actually an early attempt in that direction, apparently given the ancients' views of birth and of an unborn fetus. It was seemingly their way of taking circumstances into account when the rules were being given. We may or may not like the rule in the Exodus text, but it was an early approach to the issue. Law can be harsh. That is the reason the Courts of Equity were established in British legal history. The Judicature Act in the nineteenth century streamlined the court system in Britain, but in various states the American legal system is a very mixed bag.

As we move into the future, this issue of abortion will become more complex. We will face many questions:

- Are we willing to take into account the will of a woman in respect to her own body?
- Will we dictate to a woman how and to what extent we will regulate her body?
- What are the parameters of control?
- When does life really begin? At conception? At 15, 20, 30 or more weeks? At birth?
- Does life begin when a fetus can sustain itself without extraordinary help or when a fetal heartbeat is detected?

How do we answer these questions, and what are the implications of our answers? These questions could not have been anticipated in biblical times or even a hundred years ago. But they are present today and will be with us in the future. Christian theologians may debate them, but we need divine wisdom. And let's be honest with the questions: Does the Bible really favor, as some suggest, a "strict" anti-abortion view? Or, are our views not basically human constructs? There are no easy answers here. Humans are caught in the middle between hostile differences of opinion, and I fear that the possibilities for greater hostility among those claiming to be Christians will continue to grow. Is there room for peacemaking here, or must there be war?

Birth Control and Sexual Activity

The issue of birth control has long vexed Christians and the church. The early church interpreted the command in Genesis 1:28 to "be fruitful and multiply" as a strict rule for humanity, and restrictions on that imperative were regarded as violations of a divine ordinance. Thus, the early use of contraceptives was looked upon with disfavor by many Christians and especially in Roman Catholic and more restrictive churches who viewed contraceptives as unchristian. Even in our contemporary setting some self-proclaiming Protestant moralists are reasserting those old views and not only advising the non-use of contraceptives but also condemning those who refrain from having children as opposed to the will of God. In an agricultural society the more children one could have, the more workers (especially sons) would be available and the better it was economically for the whole family.

But society, especially in the West, has changed radically and large families are no longer regarded as desirable. In today's world, for families to be economically viable and sustainable, married women often have to work—not to mention the fact that many families depend on women to be the major wage earners. Furthermore, the development of birth control pills has virtually eliminated older methods of birth control such as the use of douches as a method for controlling fertilization or refraining from sexual activity in periods of gestation. Indeed, pills are now available for the rejection of fertilization after sexual activity. Accordingly, birth control pills have made it possible for women to work after marriage because they are able to avoid pregnancy. Thus, the pill has made birth control not only possible but also an acceptable and common practice among many Christians in society, and it has rendered as passé the old arguments in the church against birth control.

So the question emerges: Do you now hear many arguments against the easy availability of birth control pills? Once there were fairly intense debates about the pill. Perhaps there are still some debates in the minds of people over whether insurance plans should cover them, but that is a different matter. Birth control pills are here to stay, and they will become more effective and easier to use.

Yet there is another concern that arises from the easy access of such pills: the continuing rise of premarital sex—and, of course, extramarital sexual activity. When it is easy to avoid pregnancy, then age-old questions become more pertinent in the minds of people—particularly young people—such as: Is there any reason to deny committed lovers the right to engage in premarital sex? This question will continue to haunt our future generations because so-called "shotgun weddings" are becoming a thing of the past—unless young people want to prove to some family members that they want to get married. The common response today is: "If you are not protected, you are not very wise!" While issues of sexual purity and virginity are age-old issues in the church and will continue to be asserted, the restraining forces in society against sexual involvement have been considerably reduced in the current era. This change raises an important challenge for the church.

The church and Christian leaders may have to give more attention to instruction on marriage preparation and to address questions such as: Why are virginity and purity important? It will continue to be a difficult task for the church to develop adequate programs on this issue because in the past the church has generally eschewed discussing any matters of sexuality, except perhaps by way of condemnation. Sexuality has almost been an astutely avoided area of concern. Moreover, since much of the history of the church is linked to celibacy, the clergy were ill-prepared to face these issues. In addition, homosexual activity among the clergy was not unheard of in the church's history, although such activity was usually kept as a dark secret by ecclesiastical authorities.

Accordingly, the church must now take a more positive approach to sexuality and not merely stand as a judge over perceived indiscretions. It is time for a more holistic approach to this issue, and I pray that we will not be afraid in the future to deal with these concerns forthrightly and fairly. If the church cannot approach the multiple issues of sexuality without simply being judgmental, then I fear they will become irrelevant in the future.

I also think that if the church should be constantly reforming, what about our seminaries? Not many seminaries are dealing with sexuality and other issues adequately, but maybe that is where we need to begin. I realize that the response from the faculty will naturally be that we cannot add anything else to the curriculum, but maybe it is time to examine how we are preparing our ministers to deal with tough issues in their future experiences—some of which may not even be in our minds.

Will the church and Christian leaders be able to face these issues fairly and holistically? I am hopeful but the question remains open. Yet, I am convinced that if the model of Jesus is the key, then the future will be bright. Perhaps instruction in seminaries is where the training for church leaders should begin.

Genetic Engineering and Fetal Tissue

The previous issues impact another strategic issue: the use of fetal tissue. Abortions can provide fetal tissue that is useful in medical research. Although there are other ways of obtaining DNA samples, will we allow medical researchers to use fetal tissue for experiments? And what would that idea imply about a fetus and life? Such may be an important question related to improved medical treatments and the production of new medications in the future. How will we deal with such possibilities and with the many dangers lurking in medical research?

We have already developed the means for altering gene patterns in humans, for example in homosexual or bisexual or transgender persons. In the future will we move further in altering the human genetic structure? That process might possibly be used positively for altering other patterns—even of various malformations *en utero*—or negatively used by tyrants to construct some strange species of humanity. Are we prepared for new positive possibilities and possible dangers? God may have allowed us to progress in our development of possibilities to previously unimagined stages. Where are the safeguards and controls? What are the limits of our research? These questions hover around us, and we will have to face them in the future. Are we ready?

Robotics and Artificial Intelligence

Raising the question of strange species of humans adds another set of questions. Robotic equipment is already being used in many industries, but we are just at the early stages of manufactured intelligence. The possibilities at this point seem almost endless. The computer chip has revolutionized our current reality. Such a thought would probably have frightened many of our recent ancestors because they may have had an uneasy sense that in the hands of ruthless people these mechanisms would have signaled great dangers ahead such as those we might see in the *Star Wars* movies or other media presentations.

The future, of course, provides wonderful possibilities but also some not-so-inviting alternatives. Questions on the use of robotics and gene manipulations will soon face us with tornado-like winds. We need to have answers. Are we prepared to deal with these expanding possibilities? What guidelines will we set for the future of such innovations? Could ruthless governments use such inventions or discoveries to conquer other peoples and curtail their freedoms and genuine positive progress on earth—even beyond our planet? These questions beg answers!

Transplants and the Ways of the Future

The notion of transplants and the realistic idea of air and space travel or computer-generated living patterns on our earth were not even imagined in the period when the biblical texts were written. Indeed, those thoughts would have even been beyond countenance by my great-grandparents. Yet, I had a cornea transplant during the time when I was teaching in Louisville. I remember vividly that the surgeon described how the cornea was flown from Florida to Kentucky in an ice pack. The surgeon had placed my name on a preferred list so that I received the transplant earlier than others who may have also been waiting. That doctor's decision related not only to me but also to others who may have been impacted by that decision. In other words, I was the subject of a major

"Godlike" decision. I have never forgotten that fact. Moreover, that cornea was a gift from someone who needed to die in order for me to receive it, and it was transported by a special air carrier from hundreds of miles away. All of this was beyond even a dream for the biblical writers—or even a hundred years ago.

But if I thought that such a phenomenon was the limit of what might be possible in the future, I would be badly out of touch with reality. Those future realities are coming faster than we might expect, and they will soon be experienced. Indeed, I suspect that the time is coming when medical people will be able to transplant many other parts of the body, perhaps even from people who are just in the process of dying—to say nothing of the use of artificial parts for the body and beyond. I cannot even predict what will be common for my potentially unborn great-grandchildren—either for good or for evil! For them, not only is space expanding, but their patterns of travel, ways of communication, styles of living, and even food preparations will be greatly changing and expanding. Their reality could be as different as the changes from my great-grandparents to me and even more.

What then is my point? We may not understand what is coming, but we can prepare for the arrival of our great-grandchildren by assisting their parents and grandparents in preparing for the future.   Like us, the coming generations will need to place themselves in the hand of Almighty God in order to help their children trust in Christ Jesus so that they will have a sense of life and meaning beyond their immediate space-and-time realities.

To this end, will you join me in praying that wisdom, guidance, and kindness will be given to both our current and future generations—so that we and they will not face fierce storms of chaos but will realize authentic advancement and be empowered to depend upon the great hope that has been made available to all of us in Christ Jesus?

May we and those who come after us be prepared to face the future with perceptive minds and to recognize both the possibilities of progress and the dangers lurking in the misuse of resources and personnel. May all of us accept our God-given responsibility to care for our contextual universe and for all those who dwell with us in time and space until the *eschaton* (the return of Jesus) and God Almighty will bring to a conclusion all things through Christ Jesus, our Lord!

In Christian love,
Dad/Dr. B.

The Continuing Quest for Answers

A half century ago—on July 20, 1969—astronaut Neil Armstrong stepped out onto the surface of the moon and uttered those historic words: "One small step for [a] man—one giant leap for mankind." It was an event that signaled for humanity that major changes have been occurring. Never before had a mere human stood on a planetoid terrain outside of our earth. Armstrong and his companion, Buzz Aldrin, quickly became vivid symbols of the momentous—unstoppable—changes that have been taking place in our era, and they remind us that we must be prepared to view our questions about life and reality within an ever-expanding perspective.

The message of Jesus will never be out of date, but some of the perspectives of mere humans may need repeated modification to address the issues that will come before us in the future. Yes, change is inevitable. The way we view reality is not the way the early followers of Jesus did; nor those who lived during the establishment of Christendom with Constantine and Justinian; nor in the Middle Ages with Augustine and the Monastics; nor in the era of the Reformation with Luther, Calvin, and Zwingli; nor in the period of the pilgrims; nor in the events of the American Revolution; nor during the times of the modern missionary movement and the Second Great Awakening; nor in the tragedy of the Hitler era, the cataclysm of the Second World War; nor in the beginning of the atomic age—not even in the period that initiated space exploration. The cry of the later reformers—*semper reformanda* (always reforming)—must apply not only to our personal lives but also to our understandings and perspectives.

Throughout this work I have sought to lead you through a portion of the maze of questions that pummel us, seeking to arrive at some answers to important ethical and theological questions. Hopefully this journey will have encouraged you to venture forward in your pilgrimage of dealing with the many chaotic elements in the context of your world and beyond. Prayerfully this experience may also continue to assist you in more clearly focusing on the pattern of Christ in your understanding and living as Christians.

In this wrestling with options it should have become apparent that we probably do not and will not agree on all the ideas I have proposed or suggested. But I trust that one of my goals should have become quite obvious—namely, as a biblical scholar, I have tried to make my answers both biblically sound and as Christlike as possible. I have not claimed that my proposals or suggested answers are final, absolute, or inerrant. But I would posit them as among the best that I can reach, given my understanding of reality at this point in time. But the journey is not over, so please reflect with me just a little more.

Some of the answers I have proposed may not have fit your perspectives. Some may have disturbed you. Some of them may have challenged you. With some, you may have agreed or disagreed. Some may even have led you to re-evaluate your perceptions. Yet hopefully the questions have forced you to wrestle more deeply with the issues. Now, please do not be concerned or troubled if you are still undecided and do not have the answers you wish at this point. I am confident that God will lead you and all of us to Christlike resolutions—if we give our questions to the Lord! To remain tentative in evaluating some matters should not be disturbing. It merely helps us to recognize the obvious reality that we as Christians are mere mortals who are struggling for integrity and truth but are not endowed with the wisdom and knowledge of our Creator and redeemer.

I would also remind you that, as humans, we tend to differ in terms of our stations in life and the experiences that have molded our opinions and choices. Our answers may be and can be different. That is not difficult to imagine. But let me explain here what I mean by using a handy set of categories for characterizing our current generations and our wrestling with questions—being fully aware that these categories are neither firm nor complete and that not all people belong in their supposed temporal categories.

Some of our readers at this stage may be viewed as the final remnants of the old merged group frequently called the "late Boomers, Builders, and early Busters" who are now gradually passing from the scene. They grew up in an era when they tried desperately to put things together for those who would come after them and, while they were often frustrated in their efforts to achieve their goals, they have been blessed because the economy and society were booming after the Second World War and their efforts in many cases were blessed beyond their expectations.

Their children are from the next "uneasy stage of the middle and late Busters." They soon began to realize that things were changing and the booming era was passing. Life for them has had many more uncertainties, and indeed they have faced many questions. Moreover, they have been encompassed by struggles and have witnessed many evidences of narcissistic and self-centered people impacting them for ill. Uncertain situations have assailed them. Indeed, many of those who directed these self-centered patterns also have proclaimed themselves to have the answers to stability, security, and well-being in life. But those leaders have usually been badly out of touch with reality. Yet they are still among us proclaiming their false messages of utopias.

The grandchildren today face an even more difficult set of conditions in their combination era of the bewildered but determined Gen-Xer(s) and the "rudderless but seeking Millennial(s)." They are a mixed group that we sometimes call the generation Z. Sometimes they are even quite unlike their siblings. They are slowly but surely coming of age, and many of them have been grappling with the major idea of what they should be doing with their lives. Their parents are often exceedingly frustrated and may have been struggling to get some of their children even started on their journey. Yet many of those same parents may themselves be tied in disabling knots of life. So these parents and their children have contended with scores of baffling questions, not the least of which is identity.

This wrestling with questions is one reason that I, as a professor, pastor and administrator, have focused this present work on questions. I trust that you, my readers, have recognized that such questions are in fact the warp and woof of our current existence as people who are living on this planet called Earth that is swirling in the vast stretches of seemingly unending space. My responses to this plethora of questions involving the reality of chaos and indeed evil or the dark side that we have encountered is that we need help from beyond ourselves. We may be bright, but we are not omniscient. We may not be excited by the thought of dependence, but it is the one pattern that actually works. The Triune God—the Almighty Lord, our wonderful Savior, Christ Jesus, and the mysterious Holy Spirit—understand(s) both chaos and evil and is very present among us to help us deal with these frustrating questions and our repeated experiences of chaos and the dark enemy. Let me assure you that our God is not overwhelmed by either; they are not something new for the Lord. Chaos and evil are as old as creation, and some day they will surely be replaced by the new heaven and the new earth, when the former things will have passed away (Rev. 21:1-4). That is the divine promise. But in the meantime, God's Spirit remains with us as the sustaining power that enables us to deal with both our questions about life and with our debilitating ethical quandaries and issues.

Again, let me stress to you that the answer to chaos and evil is not to be found in the constructs of this world or in the grand plans of nations for success, power, and dominance. Earthly utopias may seem appealing, but in the end they are empty, narcissistic dreams of myopic proponents that ultimately leave their advocates and followers devoid of genuine meaning and hope. Authentic hope is available only through the Creator and the savior of humanity. Trusting in God and not in the plans of human leaders is the recipe for personal peace and sanity in our troubled world because our leaders are not divine. Yet we who are Christians should sincerely commit ourselves to building a better planet and to join all those who commit themselves to the care of our earthly globe, indeed the universe, and to the building of a better community among all mortals. And as Jesus showed by example, we must not overlook the weak among us—those of the vast majority who populate our world and are desperately in need of help. God does not expect us to sit on the sidelines and merely wait on an external divine solution to answer our concerns while darkness and chaos are rampant and seem to prevail. We as Christians can be powerful agents of the loving God to bring about a greater presence of truth, peace, kindness, goodness, integrity, joy, and above all else love in our world because we know the author of these authentic qualities (cf. Gal. 5:22).

Our questions will persist as long as chaos and evil exist. But if we commit ourselves to Christ and to seeking God's will, we will be in for some marvelous surprises. Of this fact I am confident because the Creator of our vast reality can use us who are "living sacrifices" to accomplish divine purposes (Rom. 12:1) that will astound us who are empowered to be the agents of the Almighty.

Thank you, then, for accompanying me on our journey of wrestling with these crucial questions that regularly confront Christians as we seek to be Christlike in answering and responding to the dilemmas of life. But I remind you again that your journey is not complete when you have finished reading this book. As long as God gives each of us breath, the journey continues because we are called to be the foretaste of the New Creation—we are Christ's ambassadors who are called to serve as reconcilers in our troubled world (2 Cor. 5:17-21).

May we purposefully accept that calling as God's agents who look beyond our contexts of chaos and never forget the incisive words of our Lord Jesus who said: "Pay attention, I am with you always until the end of created time!" (Matt. 28:20).

Our answer should be: "Thanks, be to God!"

Dad/Dr. B.

Index